KT-455-760

LAN-ANH BUI & JOSEPHINE WAN

Amigurumi

GUILD OF MASTER CRAFTSMAN PUBLICATIONS

Dedications

Josephine: to Mummy, Sam and Lewis
Lan-Anh: to my mother and Vi for their patience

First published 2010 by
Guild of Master Craftsman Publications Ltd
Castle Place, 166 High Street,
Lewes, East Sussex BN7 1XU

Reprinted 2010, 2011, 2012 (twice)

Text and designs © Lan-Anh Bui and Josephine Wan, 2010
Copyright in the Work © GMC Publications Ltd, 2010

ISBN 978-1-86108-674-7

All rights reserved

The rights of Lan-Anh Bui and Josephine Wan to be identified
as the authors of this work has been asserted in accordance
with the Copyright Designs and Patents Act 1988, sections 77
and 78.

No part of this publication may be reproduced, stored in a
retrieval system or transmitted in any form or by any means
without the prior permission of the publisher and copyright
owner.

This book is sold subject to the condition that all designs are
copyright and are not for commercial reproduction without
the permission of the designer and copyright owner.

The publishers and authors can accept no legal responsibility
for any consequences arising from the application of
information, advice or instructions given in this publication.

A catalogue record for this book is available from
the British Library.

Charts by Gina Alton.
Pattern checking by Alison Howard.

Publisher: Jonathan Bailey
Production Manager: Jim Bulley
Managing Editor: Gerrie Purcell
Editor: Alison Howard
Managing Art Editor: Gilda Pacitti
Design: Ginny Zeal
Photography: Rebecca Mothersole

Set in Gill Sans

Colour origination by GMC Reprographics
Printed and bound in China by Hung Hing Printing Co. Ltd

Amigurumi

Why we love Amigurumi

THE AIM OF THIS BOOK is to offer an insight into the art of Amigurumi, and to take you through easy projects with step-by-step guidance to give you the confidence to move on to more advanced projects.

If you are an absolute beginner to crochet, it is worth spending some time practising basic techniques such as the magic circle, double crochet, increasing and decreasing. Once you have mastered these skills, you can move from project to project as you wish, creating anything from cute egg bunnies to the fiercest dinosaur!

We have also embellished our creations to try to offer an insight into the endless possibilities of beads, felt and thread. Every one of our patterns is highly adaptable to suit the recipient: for example, if the toy is intended for a young child, beads may not be ideal. In this case, you can simply crochet or embroider a simple substitute.

We, and our families, have spent many hours planning the designs, colours, and instructions in this book. We have taken inspiration from many different sources and hope we can pass this inspiration on to you, so that you may embark on these projects with a degree of passion that matches our own.

We love Amigurumi because it is based on very simple techniques, but the completed projects are amazing. We wanted to share the joy of a hobby that is all gain and very little pain, and we hope that you have as much fun with this book as we have had creating it.

Lan-Anh and Josephine

Contents

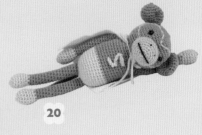

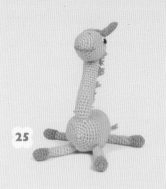

25

26

27

28

29

30

These fun characters are a really simple introduction to Amigurumi, but so cuddly that everybody will want one. Vary the shades of yarn to make each one different – it's a great way to use up oddments.

Egg Bear

Materials

Debbie Bliss Cashmerino Aran 55% merino wool
33% microfibre 12% cashmere (90m per 50g)
Oddment in shade A
Oddment in shade B
3mm crochet hook
Black embroidery yarn
Safety eyes or black beads
Toy stuffing
Small piece of felt and fabric adhesive (optional)

Special techniques

Magic circle (MC)
Double crochet (dc)
Increasing
Decreasing

Size

2½in (6cm) high

Ears (make 2)

Round 1: Using the magic circle technique (MC) and B, work 4 dc. 4 sts

Round 2: 2dc into each st. 8 sts

Round 3–4: Dc around. 8 sts

Break yarn, leaving a long tail.

Round	Stitches	Yarn
1	MC 4	B
2	8 (inc 4)	B
3–4	8 (inc 4)	B

Body (make 1)

Round 1: Using MC and A, work 6 dc. 6 sts

Round 2: 2dc into each st. 12 sts

Round 3: (2dc in next dc, dc in next dc) rep around. 18 sts

Round 4: (2dc in next dc, dc in next 2 dc) rep around. 24 sts

Round 5: (2dc in next dc, dc in next 3 dc) rep around. 30 sts

Round 6: Dc around. 30 sts

Round 7: (2dc in next dc, dc in next 4 dc) rep around. 36 sts

Rounds 8–13: Dc around. 36 sts

Change to B.

Rounds 14–17: Dc around. 36 sts

Round 18: (dc in next 4 dc, dc2tog) rep around. 30 sts

Round 19: (dc in next 3 dc, dc2tog) rep around. 24 sts

Round 20: Dc around. 24 sts

Round 21: (dc in next 2dc, dc2tog) rep around. 18 sts

Stuff toy.

Continue in rounds to close top.

Round 22: (dc in next dc, dc2tog) rep around. 12 sts

Round 23: (dc2tog) rep around. 6 sts

Break yarn, leaving a long tail.

Round	Stitches	Yarn
1	MC 6	A
2	12 (inc 6)	A
3	18 (inc 6)	A
4	24 (inc 6)	A
5	30 (inc 6)	A
6	30	A
7	36 (inc 6)	A
8–13	36	A
14–17	36	B
18	30 (dec 6)	B
19	24 (dec 6)	B
20	24	B
21	18 (dec 6)	B
Stuff toy		
22	12 (dec 6)	B
23	6 (dec 6)	B

Making up

Using yarn tails attach ears to body, 5 rounds down from centre. Attach safety eyes or beads between rounds 9 and 10, leaving 10 sts between. Cut a felt oval for the muzzle and embroider nose and mouth on it. Attach muzzle between eyes using adhesive, or sew in place.

Safety note

If the toy is to be used by a child, ensure that the eyes are very securely attached. If you prefer a washable toy, omit the felt muzzle and embroider the nose and mouth directly on the toy.

This trio of cheeky characters make ideal mobile phone charms or key rings. They are really simple and fast to work, so you'll soon be making them for all your friends.

Charm School

Materials

Debbie Bliss Cashmerino Aran 55% merino wool 33% microfibre 12% cashmere (90m per 50g)

Panda: 10g in each of black and white

Frog: 10g green

Lion: 10g yellow and 10g orange

Small piece of black felt for panda

Small piece of yellow felt for lion

Toy eyes (optional)

For all charms

2.5mm crochet hook

Black embroidery yarn

Toy stuffing

Key/phone charm strap

Size

1½in (4cm) high

PANDA
Head (make 1)

Round 1: Using white and MC, work 7 dc. 7 sts

Round 2: 2dc into each st. 14 sts

Round 3: (2dc in next dc, dc in next dc) rep around. 21 sts

Round 4: Dc around. 21 sts

Round 5: (2dc in next dc, dc in next 6 dc) rep around. 24 sts

Rounds 6–9: Dc around. 24 sts

Round 10: (dc in next 6 dc, dc2tog) rep around. 21 sts

Round 11: (dc in next dc, dc2tog) rep around. 14 sts

Stuff toy and attach charm strap to top of head. Cut 2 felt ovals and attach to head between rounds 6–7. Using black thread, embroider eyes over felt, or attach safety eyes.

Round 12: Dc2tog; rep around. 7 sts
Sew hole to close.

Round	Stitches	Yarn
1	MC 7	white
2	14 (inc 7)	white
3	21 (inc 7)	white
4	21	white
5	24 (inc 3)	white
6–9	24	white
10	21 (dec 3)	white
11	14 (dec 7)	white
Attach charm strap to top of head. Cut felt ovals and attach to head between rounds 6–7. Add eyes.		
12	7 (dec 7)	white

Ears (make 2)

Round 1: Using black and MC, work 4 dc. 4 sts

Round 2: Dc around. 4 sts

Round	Stitches	Yarn
1	MC 4	black
2	4	black

Making up

Attach ears to head, beginning from round 2. Sew on tail.

Head (make 1)

Round 1: Using green and MC, work 9 dc. 9 sts

Round 2: 2 dc into each st. 18 sts

Round 3: (2dc in next dc, dc in next dc) rep around. 27 sts

Round 4: Dc around. 27 sts

Round 5: (2dc in next dc, dc in next 8 dc) rep around. 30 sts

Rounds 6–9: Dc around. 30 sts

Round 10: (dc in next 8 dc, dc2tog) rep around. 27 sts

Round 11: (dc in next dc, dc2tog) rep around. 18 sts

Attach strap to top of head. Sew on eyes, beg from round 2. Stuff toy.

Round 12: (dc2tog) rep around. 9 sts

Round 13: Work 2 sts into 1 until hole closes.

FROG
Eyes (make 2)

Round 1: Using MC and green, work 5 dc. 5 sts

Round 2: 2dc into each st. 10 sts

Round 3: Work 1 st of round., then break yarn, leaving a long tail.

Round	Stitches	Yarn
1	MC 5	green
2	10 (inc 5)	green
3	1 (1 st only)	green

Round	Stitches	Yarn
1	MC 9	green
2	18 (inc 9)	green
3	27 (inc 9)	green
4	27	green
5	30 (inc 7)	green
6–9	30	green
10	27 (dec 3)	green
11	18 (dec 9)	green
Attach strap and embroider face. Sew on eyes. Stuff toy.		
12	9 (dec 9)	green
13	2 sts into 1 until hole closes	green

LION
Head (make 1)

Round 1: Using yellow and MC, work 7 dc. 7 sts

Round 2: 2dc into each st. 14 sts

Round 3: (2dc in next dc, dc into next 2 dc) to end. 21 sts

Round 4: Dc around. 21 sts

Rounds 5–9: (2dc into next dc, dc into next 6 dc) to end. 24 sts

Round 10: (dc in next 6 dc, dc2tog) rep around. 21 sts

Round 11: (dc in next dc, dc2tog) rep around. 14 sts

Attach strap to top of head. Sew on eyes between rounds 5 and 6, approx 7 sts apart. Stuff toy.

Round 12: Dc2tog; rep around. 7 sts

Round 13: Work 2 sts into 1 until hole closes.

Ears (make 2)

Round 1: Using yellow and MC, work 2 dc. 2 sts

Round 2: Work 2 sts into 1. Break yarn, leaving a long tail. Attach ears, beg from round 2.

Mane

Using B, sew loops all round head to form mane.

Round	Stitches	Yarn
1	MC 7	yellow
2	14 (inc 7)	yellow
3	21 (inc 7)	yellow
4	21	yellow
5	24 (inc 3)	yellow
6–9	24	yellow
10	21 (dec 3)	yellow
11	14 (dec 7)	yellow
Attach strap and embroider face		
12	7 (dec 7)	yellow
13+	2 sts into 1 until hole closes	yellow

These quirky toys are really fast to work, and look just like yummy cakes – until you notice their cheeky faces. Make each face slightly different to give these little bears their own personalities.

Cupcake bear

Materials

Debbie Bliss Baby Cashmerino 4-ply 55% merino wool 33% microfibre 12% cashmere (125m per 50g)
1 x 50g ball shade A
1 x 50g ball shade B
3mm crochet hook
Safety eyes
Black embroidery thread
Toy stuffing
Oddment of white felt

Special techniques

Magic circle (MC)
Double crochet (dc)
Increasing
Decreasing
Slip stitch (sl st)

Size

2½in (6cm) across

Base

Round 1: Using A and MC, work 7 dc. 7 sts

Round 2: 2dc into each st. 14 sts

Round 3: (2dc in next dc, dc in next dc) rep around. 21 sts

Round 4: (2dc in next dc, dc in next 2 dc) rep around. 28 sts

Round 5: Work 28 dc into back of sts of round 4. 28 sts

Rounds 6–10: Dc around. 28 sts
Break yarn leaving a long tail, sl st to join and pull tail through loop.

Frosting

Round 1: Using B and MC, work 7 dc. 7 sts

Round 2: 2 dc into each st. 14 sts

Round 3: (2dc in next dc, dc in next dc) rep around. 21 sts

Round 4: Dc around. 21 sts

Round 5: (2dc in next dc, dc in next 2 dc) rep around. 28 sts

Rounds 6–8: Dc around. 28 sts

Round 9: ([1 dc, 2 ch, 1 dc] in next dc, sl st in next dc) rep to last dc.
Break yarn, leaving a long tail.

Making up

Attach eyes and cut fabric piece into a small muzzle shape. Sew muzzle to frosting. Embroider nose and mouth. Attach frosting to base, leaving a 1in (2.5cm) opening for stuffing. Stuff toy and finish sewing frosting to base.

Round	Stitches	Yarn
1	MC 7	A
2	14 (inc 7)	A
3	21 (inc 7)	A
4	28 (inc 7)	A
5	28 into back of sts	A
6–10	28	A

Round	Stitches	Yarn
1	MC 7	B
2	14 (inc 7)	B
3	21 (inc 7)	B
4	21	B
5	28 (inc 7)	B
6–8	28	B
9	edging	B

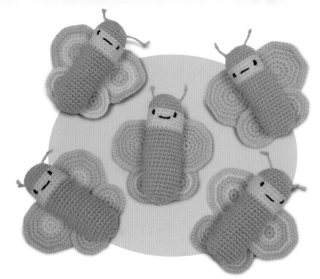

Let your imagination run riot with these colourful characters, which can be made in any combination of colours. Attach several butterflies to a simple frame – or even a coathanger – to make a wonderful mobile.

Fabulous Flutterby

Materials

Debbie Bliss Cashmerino Aran 55% merino wool
33% microfibre 12% cashmere (90m per 50g ball)
1 x 50g ball beige (A)
1 x 50g ball white (B)
Oddments of same yarn in contrasting shades (C and D)
2.5mm and 3mm crochet hooks
Oddment of yarn to embroider face

Special techniques

Magic circle (MC)
Double crochet (dc)

Size

3in (7.5cm) high

Note

The quantity of main yarn given makes 5 butterflies.

Head and body (make 1)

Round 1: Using 3mm hook, MC and A, work 8 dc. 8 sts

Round 2: 2dc into each st. 16 sts

Round 3: (2dc in next dc, dc in next dc) rep around. 24 sts

Rounds 4–6: Dc in each dc to end. 24 sts Change to B.

Rounds 7–11: Dc around. 24 sts Change to A.

Rounds 12–28: Dc around. 24 sts

Round 29: (dc in next dc, dc2tog) to end. 18 sts

Round 30: As round 29. 9 sts. Stuff toy.

Next round: Work 2 sts into 1 until hole closes.

Break yarn and sew in tail.

Round	Stitches	Yarn
1	MC 8	A
2	16 (inc 8)	A
3	24 (inc 8)	A
4–6	24	A
Embroider face		
7–11	24	B
12–28	24	A
29	18 (dec 6)	A
30	9 (dec 9)	A

Large wings (make 2)

Round 1: Using C and MC, work 8 dc. 8 sts
Change to D.
Round 2: 2dc into each st. 16 sts
Change to C.
Round 3: (2dc in next dc, dc in next dc) rep around. 24 sts
Change to D.
Round 4: (2dc in next dc, dc in next 2dc) rep around. 32 sts
Change to C.
Round 5: As round 4. 40 sts
Change to D.
Round 6: As round 5. 48 sts
Break yarn and sew in tail.

Round	Stitches	Yarn
1	MC 8	C
2	16 (inc 8)	D
3	24 (inc 8)	C
4	32 (inc 8)	D
5	40 (inc 8)	C
6	48 (inc 8)	D

Note

Wings may be made in any two colours. These are referred to in the instructions as C and D.

Small wings (make 2)

Round 1: Using 3mm hook, D and MC, work 8 dc. 8 sts
Round 2: 2dc into each st. 16 sts
Change to C.
Round 3: (2dc in next dc, dc in next dc) rep around. 24 sts
Round 4: (3dc in next dc, dc in next 2 dc) rep around. 32 sts
Break yarn and sew in tail.

Round	Stitches	Yarn
1	MC 8	D
2	16 (inc 8)	D
3	24 (inc 8)	C
4	32 (inc 8)	C

Making up

Join the sides of the two large wings for approx 8 sts. Join sides of the two small wings for approx 5 sts. Attach wings to back of body and trim off excess yarn. Embroider the eyes and mouth between rounds 6 and 7.

Antennae (make 2)

Knot the end of a length of yarn A. Cut off about 4in (10cm) and sew through head. Knot the other end and trim off any excess yarn.

This little chap is an unusual toy
that is sure to bring a smile to anyone's face.
In fact, you could say that he really is a fun guy!

Fergus Fungus

Materials

DB Cashmerino Aran 55% merino wool 33% microfibre
12% cashmere (90m per 50g)
25g red (A)
Acrylic DK yarn
Oddment of white (B)
3mm crochet hook
Black embroidery yarn
White felt
Toy stuffing
Toy eyes (optional)

Special techniques

Magic circle (MC)
Double crochet (dc)
Increasing
Decreasing
Blanket stitch

Size

4in (10cm) high

Base (make 1)

Round 1: Using B and MC, work 7 dc. 7 sts

Round 2: 2dc into each st. 14 sts

Round 3: (2dc in next dc, dc in next dc) rep around. 21 sts

Round 4: (2dc in next dc, dc in next 2 dc) rep around. 28 sts

Rounds 5–13: Dc around. 28 sts

Round 14: (dc in next 5 dc, dc2tog) rep around. 24 sts

Round 15: (dc in next 4 dc, dc2tog) rep around. 20 sts
Break yarn.

Round	Stitches	Yarn
1	MC 7	B
2	14 (inc 7)	B
3	21 (inc 7)	B
4	28 (inc 7)	B
5–13	28	B
14	24 (dec 4)	B
15	20 (dec 4)	B

Top (make 1)

Round 1: Using A and MC, work 7 dc. 7 sts

Round 2: 2dc into each st. 14 sts

Round 3: (2dc in next dc, dc in next dc) rep around. 21 sts

Round 4: (2dc in next dc, dc in next 2 dc) rep around. 28 sts

Round 5: (2dc in next dc, dc in next 3 dc) rep around. 35 sts

Round 6: (2dc in next dc, dc in next 4 dc) rep around. 42 sts

Rounds 7–14: Dc around. 42 sts

Round 15: (dc in next 4dc, dc2tog) rep around. 35 sts

Round 16: (dc in next 3dc, dc2tog) rep around. 28 sts

Round 17: Dc2tog (dc in next 4 dc, dc2tog) rep around, dc2tog. 22 sts
Break yarn.

Round	Stitches	Yarn
1	MC 7	A
2	14 (inc 7)	A
3	21 (inc 7)	A
4	28 (inc 7)	A
5	35 (inc 7)	A
6	42 (inc 7)	A
7–14	42	A
15	35 (dec 7)	A
16	28 (dec 7)	A
17	20 (dec 8)	A

Making up

Cut small circles from felt and sew to top of mushroom. Embroider face on stalk as shown. Stuff toy. Sew base to top of mushroom.

Note

If you prefer not to use felt, crochet circles using white yarn and the magic circle technique and attach them to the mushroom.

It's true that many gardeners don't like snails — but this cheerful gastropod may change all that. He's not interested in eating anyone's prize vegetables, but only in spreading a bit of colour and fun.

Sidney Snail

Materials

Debbie Bliss Cashmerino Aran 55% merino wool
33% microfibre 12% cashmere (90m per 50g)
25g white (A)
10g each of two contrast shades (C1 and C2)
3mm crochet hook
Pink embroidery yarn
Toy eyes
Polyester stuffing

Special techniques

Magic circle (MC)
Double crochet (dc)
Increasing
Decreasing

Size

5in (12.5cm) long

Shell (make 2)

Round 1: Using C1 and MC, work 5 dc. 5 sts

Round 2: 2dc into each st. 10 sts Change to C2.

Round 3: (2dc in next dc, dc in next dc) rep around. 15 sts Change to C1.

Round 4: (2dc in next dc, dc in next 2dc) rep around. 20 sts Change to C2.

Round 5: (2dc in next dc, dc in next 3dc) rep around. 25 sts Change to C1.

Round 6: (2dc in next dc, dc in next 4dc) rep around. 30 sts Change to C2.

Round 7: Dc around. 30 sts Change to C1.

Round 8: Dc around. 30 sts

Break yarn, leaving a long tail. WS facing, sew halves of shell together. Stuff toy and close hole. Sew in yarn ends.

Round	Stitches	Yarn
1	MC 5	C1
2	10 (inc 5)	C1
3	15 (inc 5)	C2
4	20 (inc 5)	C1
5	25 (inc 5)	C2
6	30 (inc 5)	C1
7	30	C2
8	30	C1

Head

Round 1: Using A and MC, work 5 dc. 5 sts

Round 2: 2dc into each st. 10 sts

Round 3: (2dc in next dc, dc in next dc) rep around. 15 sts

Round 4: (2dc in next dc, dc in next 2dc) rep around. 20 sts

Round 5: (2dc in next dc, dc in next 3dc) rep around. 25 sts

Rounds 6–7: Dc around. 25 sts

Rou nd 8: (dc in next 3 dc, dc2tog) rep around. 20 sts

Round 9: (dc in next 2 dc, dc2tog) rep around. 15 sts

Attach eyes and embroider mouth. Stuff toy.

Round 10: (dc in next dc, dc2tog) rep around. 10 sts

Round 11: (dc2tog) rep around. 5 sts

Round 12: Work 2 sts into 1 until hole closes.

Break yarn, leaving a long tail.

Round	Stitches	Yarn
1	MC 5	A
2	10 (inc 5)	A
3	15 (inc 5)	A
4	20 (inc 5)	A
5	25 (inc 5)	A
6–7	25	A
8	20 (dec 5)	A
9	15 (dec 5)	A
Attach eyes, embroider mouth and stuff		
10	10 (dec 5)	A
11	5 (dec 5)	A
12	2sts into 1	A

Body

Round 1: Using A and MC, work 4 dc. 4 sts

Round 2: 2dc into each st. 8 sts

Round 3: (2dc in next dc, dc in next dc) rep around. 12 sts

Rounds 4–25: Dc around. 12 sts

Stuff body lightly. Wind shell round and join to body.

Round	Stitches	Yarn
1	MC 4	A
2	8 (inc 4)	A
3	12 (inc 4)	A
4–25	12	A

Horns (make 2)

Round 1: Using A and MC, work 4 dc. 4 sts

Round 2: 2dc into each st. 8 sts

Round 3: (dc in next dc, dc2tog) rep around. 4 sts

Break yarn, leaving a long tail.

Round	Stitches	Yarn
1	MC 4	A
2	8 (inc 4)	A
3	4 (dec 4)	A

Making up

Sew horns to head and attach head to body.

This gorgeous design has so many possibilities:
a crazy toy, a pretty hanging decoration or even an air freshener
if you stuff it with fragrant pot pourri.

Berry Nice

Materials

Debbie Bliss Cashmerino Aran 55% merino wool
33% microfibre 12% cashmere (90m per 50g)

1 x 50g ball red (A)

Oddment of green (B)

3.5mm and 5mm crochet hooks

Pot pourri or toy stuffing

Safety eyes (optional)

Black embroidery thread (optional)

Special techniques

Magic circle (MC)

Double crochet (dc)

Increasing

Decreasing

Chain stitch

Size

3in (7.5cm) high

Strawberries (make 2)

Use yarn double throughout.

Round 1: Using 5mm hook, A and MC, work 5 dc. 5 sts

Round 2: 2dc into each st. 10 sts

Round 3: (2dc in next dc, dc in next dc) rep around. 15 sts

Round 4: Dc around. 15 sts

Round 5: (2dc in next dc, dc in next 2 dc) rep around. 20 sts

Round 6: Dc around. 20 sts

Round 7: (2dc in next dc, dc in next 3 dc) rep around. 25 sts

Rounds 8–9: Dc around. 25 sts

Round 10: (dc in next 3dc, dc2tog) rep around. 20 sts

Round 11: (dc in next 2dc, dc2tog) rep around. 15 sts

Round 12: Dc around. 15 sts

Round 13: (dc in next dc, dc2tog) rep around. 10 sts

Stuff with pot pourri or toy stuffing. Attach toy eyes if desired.

Round 14: Dec by working 2 sts into 1 until hole closes.

Break yarn and darn in end.

Round	Stitches	Yarn
1	MC 5	A
2	10 (inc 5)	A
3	15 (inc 5)	A
4	15	A
5	20 (inc 5)	A
6	20	A
7	25 (inc 5)	A
8–9	25	A
10	20	A
11	15 (dec 5)	A
12	15	A
13	10 (dec 5)	A
Stuff toy. Attach eyes if required.		
14	2 into 1	A

Leaf frill (make 2)

Round 1: Using 3.5mm hook, B and MC, work 6 dc. 6 sts

Round 2: 2dc into each st. 12 sts

Round 3: (2dc in next dc, dc in next dc) rep around. 18 sts

Round 4: (2dc in next dc, dc in next 2dc) rep around. 24 sts

Round 5: Dc into first st, ch4, sl st into st 2 of round.

Attach leaf frill to top of strawberry.

Round	Stitches	Yarn
1	MC 6	B
2	12 (inc 6)	B
3	18 (inc 6)	B
4	24 (inc 6)	B
5	Dc into st 1, 4ch, sl st into st 2	B

Stalk

Round 1: Using B and 3.5mm hook, work 25ch. 25 sts

Attach one end to each strawberry.

Round	Stitches	Yarn
1	25ch	B

This easily worked and unusual toy can be made in a kaleidoscope of colours. Why not use up all your oddments and make enough fishy friends to fill a fun aquarium?

Funky Fish

Materials

Araucania Pomaire 100% hand-dyed pima cotton
(168m per 50g)
1 x 50g ball variegated pink (A)
1 x 50g ball orange (B)
3mm crochet hook
Black embroidery yarn
Toy eyes
Polyester stuffing

Special techniques

Magic circle technique (MC)
Double crochet (dc)
Chain stitch (ch)
Increasing
Decreasing

Size

5in (12.5cm) long

Body

Round 1: Using A and MC, work 4 dc. 4 sts

Round 2: 2dc into each st. 8 sts

Round 3: (2dc in next dc, dc in next dc) rep around. 12 sts

Round 4: (2dc in next dc, dc in next 2 dc) rep around. 16 sts

Round 5: (2dc in next dc, dc in next 3 dc) rep around. 20 sts

Round 6: (2dc in next dc, dc in next 4 dc) rep around. 24 sts

Round 7: (2dc in next dc, dc in next 5 dc) rep around. 28 sts

Round 8: (2dc in next dc, dc in next 6 dc) rep around. 32 sts

Round 9: (2dc in next dc, dc in next 7 dc) rep around. 36 sts

Rounds 10–15: Dc around. 36 sts

Round 16: (dc in next 16 dc, dc2tog) rep around. 34 sts

Round 17: (dc in next 15 dc, dc2tog) rep around. 32 sts

Round 18: (dc in next 14 dc, dc2tog) rep around. 30 sts

Round 19: (dc in next 13 dc, dc2tog) rep around. 28 sts

Round 20: (dc in next 5 dc, dc2tog) rep around. 24 sts

Round 21: Dc around. 24 sts

Round 22: (dc in next 4 dc, dc2tog) rep around. 20 sts

Round 23: (dc in next 3 dc, dc2tog) rep around. 16 sts

Rounds 24–26: Dc around. 16 sts
Break yarn. and sew up end to close.

Round	Stitches	Yarn
1	MC 4	A
2	8 (inc 4)	A
3	12 (inc 4)	A
4	16 (inc 4)	A
5	20 (inc 4)	A
6	24 (inc 4)	A
7	28 (inc 4)	A
8	32 (inc 4)	A
9	36 (inc 4)	A
10–15	36	A
16	34 (dec 2)	A
17	32 (dec 2)	A
18	30 (dec 2)	A
19	28 (dec 2)	A
20	24 (dec 4)	A
21	24	A
22	20 (dec 4)	A
23	16 (dec 4)	A
24–26	16	A

Eyepieces (make 2)

Round 1: Using B and MC, work 4 dc. 4 sts

Round 2: 2 dc into each st. 8 sts

Round 3: (2dc in next dc, dc in next dc) rep around. 12 sts

Edging: Work (2ch, dc into next st) x 7 to form a decorative edge.

Round	Stitches	Yarn
1	MC 4	B
2	8 (inc 4)	B
3	12 (inc 4)	B

Side fins (make 2)

Round 1: Using B and MC, work 4 dc. 4 sts

Round 2: 2dc in each st. 8 sts

Round 3: (2dc in next dc, dc in next dc) rep around. 12 sts

Round 4: Dc around. 12 sts

Round 5: (dc in next 4 dc, dc2tog) rep around. 10 sts

Round 6: Dc around. 10 sts

Round 7: (dc in next 3 dc, dc2tog) rep around. 8 sts

Round 8: Dc around. 8 sts
Break yarn, leaving a long tail.
Sew fin to side of body.

Round	Stitches	Yarn
1	MC 4	B
2	8 (inc 4)	B
3	12 (inc 4)	B
4	12	B
5	10 (dec 2)	B
6	10	B
7	8 (dec 2)	B
8	8	B

Top fin

Round 1: Using B and MC, work 5 dc.
5 sts

Round 2: 2dc into each st. 10 sts

Round 3: 1ch, turn (dc in next 2 dc,
2dc in next dc) rep 4 times. 12 sts

Round 4: (2ch, dc in next dc) rep
12 times. 24 sts

Break yarn, leaving a long tail.
Attach fin to top of body.

Round	Stitches	Yarn
1	MC 5	B
2	10 (inc 5)	B
3	12	B
4	24	B

Tail fin

Round 1: Using B, work 8dc into end
of body (where hole was closed). 8 sts

Round 2: 3dc into each st. 24 sts

Round 3: 3dc into each st. 72 sts

Break yarn and sew in tail.

Round	Stitches	Yarn
1	8	B
2	24 (inc 16)	B
3	72 (inc 48)	B

Making up

Attach eyes to eyepieces and attach to
body. Embroider mouth.

This little mouse is really fast and simple to make from a scrap of yarn. It would be a brilliant, quirky toy for a small child – or even your favourite cat.

Mini Mouse

Materials

Debbie Bliss Cashmerino Aran 55% merino wool
33% microfibre 12% cashmere (90m per 50g)
1 x 50g ball beige (A)
25g white (B)
3.5mm crochet hook ·
Safety eyes or black beads
Polyester stuffing
Pink and black embroidery thread

Special techniques

Magic circle (MC)
Double crochet (dc)
Increasing
Decreasing

Size

3in (7.5cm) long, excluding tail

Ears (make 2)

Round 1: Using MC and B, work 6 dc. 6 sts

Change to A.

Round 2: 2dc into each st. 12 sts

Round 3: (2dc in next dc, dc in next dc) rep around. 18 sts

Break yarn, leaving a long tail.

Round	Stitches	Yarn
1	MC 6	B
2	12 (inc 6)	A
3	18 (inc 6)	A

Head

Round 1: Using MC and A, work 4 dc. 4 sts

Round 2: 2dc into each st. 8 sts

Round 3: (2dc in next dc, dc in next dc) rep around. 12 sts

Round 4: (2dc in next dc, dc in next 2 dc) rep around. 16 sts

Round 5: (2dc in next dc, dc in next 3 dc) rep around. 20 sts

Round 6: (2dc in next dc, dc in next 4 dc) rep around. 24 sts

Round 7: Dc around. 24 sts

Round 8: (2dc in next dc, dc in next 5 dc) rep around. 28 sts

Round 9: (2dc in next dc, dc in next 6 dc) rep around. 32 sts

Round 10: (2dc in next dc, dc in next 7 dc) rep around. 36 sts

Rounds 11–13: Dc around. 36 sts

Round 14: (2dc in next dc, dc in next 8 dc) rep around. 40 sts

Round 15: Dc around. 40 sts

Round 16: (dc in next 6 dc, dc2tog) rep around. 35 sts

Round 17: (dc in next 5 dc, dc2tog) rep around. 30 sts

Round 18: (dc in next 4 dc, dc2tog) rep around. 25 sts

Round 19: (dc in next 3 dc, dc2tog) rep around. 20 sts

Round 20: (dc in next 2 dc, dc2tog) rep around. 15 sts

Stuff toy. Attach eyes and nose. Sew ears to 8th round from nose point.

Round 21: (dc in next dc, dc2tog) rep around. 10 sts

Round 22: (dc2tog) rep around. 5 sts

Round 23: Work 2 sts into 1 until hole closes.

Fasten off, leaving a long tail.

Round	Stitches	Yarn
1	MC 4	A
2	8 (inc 4)	A
3	12 (inc 4)	A
4	16 (inc 4)	A
5	20 (inc 4)	A
6	24 (inc 4)	A
7	24	A
8	28 (inc 4)	A
9	32 (inc 4)	A
10	36 (inc 4)	A
11–13	36	A
14	40 (inc 4)	A
15	40	A
16	35 (dec 5)	A
17	30 (dec 5)	A
18	25 (dec 5)	A
19	20 (dec 5)	A
20	15 (dec 5)	A
Stuff toy. Attach eyes, nose and ears.		
21	10 (dec 5)	A
22	5 (dec 5)	A
23	2sts into 1	A

Note

*Make a whole family of
these little mice in different colours
to use up all your oddments of yarn.*

Making up

Thread through several additional
lengths of yarn and combine with the
long tail piece. Braid to form tail and
trim to desired length. Knot ends
securely and trim.

Sunny yellow and bright white combine to make
a simple toy that is sure to become a favourite.
The red 'crown' adds a jaunty touch.

Chirpy Chick

Materials

100g Debbie Bliss Cashmerino Aran 55% merino wool
33% microfibre 12% cashmere (90m per 50g)
1 x 50g ball white (A)
1 x 50g ball yellow (B)
Approx 25g red (C)
3.5mm and 4mm crochet hooks
Safety eyes

Special techniques

Magic circle (MC)
Double crochet (dc)
Increasing
Decreasing

Size

6in (15cm) high

Head

Round 1: Using 4mm hook, A and MC, work 7 dc. 7 sts

Round 2: 2dc into each st. 14 sts

Round 3: (2dc in next dc, dc in next dc) rep around. 21 sts

Round 4: (2dc in next dc, dc in next 2 dc) rep around. 28 sts

Round 5: (2dc in next dc, dc in next 3 dc) rep around. 35 sts

Round 6: Dc around. 35 sts

Round 7: (2dc in next dc, dc in next 4 dc) rep around. 42 sts

Rounds 8–15: Dc around. 42 sts

Round 16: (dc in next 4 dc, dc2tog) rep around. 35 sts

Round 17: (dc in next 3 dc, dc2tog) rep around. 28 sts

Round 18: (dc in next 2 dc, dc2tog) rep around. 21 sts

Round 19: (dc in next 5 dc, dc2tog) rep around. 18 sts

Break yarn, leaving a long tail.

Round	Stitches	Yarn
1	MC 7	A
2	14 (inc 7)	A
3	21 (inc 7)	A
4	28 (inc 7)	A
5	35 (inc 7)	A
6	35	A
7	42 (inc 7)	A
8–15	42	A
16	35 (dec 7)	A
17	28 (dec 7)	A
18	21 (dec 7)	A
19	18 (dec 3)	A

Body

Round 1: Using 4mm hook, A and MC, work 7 dc. 7 sts

Round 2: 2dc into each st. 14 sts

Round 3: (2dc in next dc, dc in next dc) rep around. 21 sts

Round 4: (2dc in next dc, dc in next 2 dc) rep around. 28 sts

Round 5: (2dc in next dc, dc in next 3 dc) rep around. 35 sts

Rounds 6–12: Dc around. 35 sts

Round 13: (dc in next 3 dc, dc2tog) rep around. 28 sts

Round 14: (dc in next 2 dc, dc2tog) rep around. 21 sts

Round 15: Dc around. 21 sts

Round 16: (dc in next 5 dc, dc2tog) rep around. 18 sts

Break yarn, leaving a long tail.

Round	Stitches	Yarn
1	MC 7	A
2	14 (inc 7)	A
3	21 (inc 7)	A
4	28 (inc 7)	A
5	35 (inc 7)	A
6–12	35	A
13	28 (dec 7)	A
14	21 (dec 7)	A
15	21	A
16	18	A

Wings (make 2)

Round 1: Using 3.5mm hook, A and MC, work 4 dc. 4 sts

Round 2: 2dc into each dc. 8 sts

Round 3: Dc around. 8 sts

Round 4: (2dc in next dc, dc in next dc) rep around. 12 sts

Rounds 5–10: Dc around. 12 sts

Round 11: (dc in next dc, dc2tog) rep around. 8 sts

Round 12: Dc around. 8 sts

Break yarn, leaving a long tail.

Round	Stitches	Yarn
1	MC 4	A
2	8 (inc 4)	A
3	8	A
4	12 (inc 4)	A
5–10	12	A
11	8 (dec 4)	A
12	8	A

Top beak

Round 1: Using 3.5mm hook, B and MC, work 5 dc. 5 sts

Round 2: (2dc into each dc) rep around. 10 sts

Round 3: (2dc in next dc, dc in next dc) rep around. 15 sts

Round 4: (2dc in next dc, dc in next 2 dc) rep around. 20 sts

Rounds 5–8: Dc around. 20 sts

Break yarn, leaving a long tail.

Round	Stitches	Yarn
I	MC 5	B
2	10 (inc 5)	B
3	15 (inc 5)	B
4	20 (inc 5)	B
5–8	20	B

Lower beak

Round I: Using 3.5mm hook, B and MC, work 5 dc. 5 sts

Round 2: (2dc into each dc) rep around. 10 sts

Round 3: (2dc in next dc, dc in next dc) rep around. 15 sts

Round 4: (2dc in next dc, dc in next 2 dc) rep around. 20 sts

Rounds 5–7: Dc around. 20 sts
Break yarn, leaving a long tail.

Round	Stitches	Yarn
I	MC 5	B
2	10 (inc 5)	B
3	15 (inc 5)	B
4	20 (inc 5)	B
5–7	20	B

Feet (make 2)

Round I: Using 3.5mm hook, B and MC, work 5dc. 5sts

Round 2: 2dc into each st. 10 sts

Rounds 3–6: Dc around. 10 sts

Round 7: (2dc in next dc, dc in next dc) rep around. 15 sts
Break yarn, leaving a long tail.

Round	Stitches	Yarn
I	MC 5	B
2	10 (inc 5)	B
3–6	10	B
7	15 (inc 5)	B

Crown (in three parts)
Part I

Round I: Using 3.5mm hook, C and MC, work 5 dc. 5 sts

Round 2: 2dc into each st (10 sts); ch I, turn.

Round 3: (2dc in next dc, dc in next 4 dc); rep (13 sts); ch I, turn.

Round 4: (2dc in next dc, dc in next 3 dc); rep 3 times, 2dc in last dc. 17 sts
Break yarn, leaving a long tail.

Round	Stitches	Yarn
I	MC 5	C
2	10 (inc 5)	C
3	13 (inc 3)	C
4	17 (inc 4)	C

Part 2

Round I: Using 3.5mm hook, C and MC, work 5 dc. 5 sts

Round 2: 2dc into each st (10 sts) make 1ch, turn.

Round 3: 2dc in next dc, dc in next 4 dc); rep to end. 13 sts
Break yarn, leaving a long tail.

Round	Stitches	Yarn
I	MC 5	C
2	10 (inc 5)	C
3	13 (inc 3)	C

Part 3

Round I: Using C and MC, work 5 dc. 5 sts

Round 2: 2dc into each st. 10 sts
Break yarn, leaving long tail.

Round	Stitches	Yarn
I	MC 5	C
2	10 (inc 5)	C

Tail

Using B, work as for feet.

Making up

Attach eyes between rounds 11 and 12, approx 10 sts apart. Join beak sections and attach to head. Attach crown pieces to head and stuff head. Stuff feet and embroider toes if required. Attach feet and sew on wings. Stuff body and attach to head. Attach tail to back of lower body.

The cutest of baby bunnies will make the perfect gift
for a new baby, a small child, or anyone who loves rabbits,
if you can bear to part with it yourself!

Baby Bunny

Materials

Debbie Bliss Cashmerino Aran 55% merino wool
33% microfibre 12% cashmere (90m per 50g)
1 x 50g ball main shade (A)
Oddment in contrasting shade (B)
3mm crochet hook
Embroidery thread in black and white
Toy stuffing
Safety eyes
Novelty button

Special techniques

Magic circle (MC)
Double crochet (dc)
Increasing
Decreasing

Size

7in (18cm) tall

Ears (make 2)

Round 1: Using A and MC, work 4 dc. 4 sts

Round 2: (2dc in next dc, dc in next dc) rep around. 6 sts

Round 3: (2dc in next dc, dc in next 2 dc) rep around. 8 sts

Round 4: Dc around. 8 sts

Round 5: (2dc in next dc, dc in next 3 dc) rep around. 10 sts

Round 6: Dc around. 10 sts

Round 7: (dc in next 3 dc, dc2tog) rep around. 8 sts

Round 8: Dc around. 8 sts

Round 9: (dc in next 2 dc, dc2tog) rep around. 6 sts

Break yarn, leaving a long tail.

Round	Stitches	Yarn
1	MC 4	A
2	6 (inc 2)	A
3	8 (inc 2)	A
4	8	A
5	10 (inc 2)	A
6	10	A
7	8 (dec 2)	A
8	8	A
9	6 (dec 2)	A

Head

Round 1: Using A and MC, work 8 dc. 8 sts

Round 2: 2dc into each st. 16 sts

Round 3: (2dc in next dc, dc in next dc) rep around. 24 sts

Round 4: (2dc in next dc, dc in next 3 dc) rep around. 32 sts

Round 5: (2dc in next dc, dc in next 5 dc) rep around. 40 sts

Rounds 6–12: Dc around. 40 sts

Round 13: (dc in next 3 dc, dc2tog) rep around. 32 sts

Round 14: (dc in next 2 dc, dc2tog) rep around. 24 sts

Round 15: (dc in next dc, dc2tog) rep around. 16 sts

Break yarn, leaving a long tail.

Round	Stitches	Yarn
1	MC 8	A
2	16 (inc 8)	A
3	24 (inc 8)	A
4	32 (inc 8)	A
5	40	A
6	40 (inc 8)	A
7–12	40	A
13	32 (dec 8)	A
14	24 (dec 8)	A
15	16 (dec 8)	A

Body

Round 1: Using A and MC, work 8 dc. 8 sts

Round 2: 2dc into each st. 16 sts

Round 3: (2dc in next dc, dc in next dc) rep around. 24 sts

Round 4: (2dc in next dc, dc in next 2 dc) rep around. 32 sts

Round 5: (dc in next 7dc, 2dc in next dc). 36 sts

Rounds 6–7: Dc around. 36 sts
Change to B.

Rounds 8–9: Dc around. 36 sts

Round 10: (dc in next 7 dc, dc2tog) rep around. 32 sts

Round 11: Dc around. 32 sts

Round 12: (dc in next 2 dc, dc2tog) rep around. 24 sts

Round 13: Dc around. 24 sts

Round 14: (dc in next dc, dc2tog) rep around. 18 sts

Break yarn, leaving a long tail.

Round	Stitches	Yarn
1	MC8	A
2	16 (inc 8)	A
3	24 (inc 8)	A
4	32 (inc 8)	A
5	36 (inc 4)	A
6–7	36	A
Change to B		
8–9	36	B
10	32 (dec 4)	B
11	32	B
12	24 (dec 8)	B
13	24	B
14	18 (dec 6)	B

Arms (make 2)

Round 1: Using A and MC, work 5 dc. 5 sts

Rounds 2–4: 2dc into each st. 10 sts Change to B.

Round 5: Dc around. 10 sts

Round 6: (dc in next 3 dc, dc2tog) rep around. 8 sts

Rounds 7–8: Dc around. 8 sts Break yarn, leaving a long tail.

Round	Stitches	Yarn
1	MC 5	A
2	10 (inc 5)	A
3–4	10	A
5	10	B
6	8 (dec 2)	B
7–8	8	B

Legs (make 2)

Round 1: Using A and MC, work 5 dc. 5 sts

Round 2: 2dc into each st. 10 sts

Rounds 3–6: Dc around. 10 sts

Round 7: (dc in next 3 dc, dc2tog) rep around. 8 sts

Round 8: Dc around. 8 sts Break yarn, leaving a long tail.

Round	Stitches	Yarn
1	MC 5	A
2	10 (inc 5)	A
3–6	10	A
7	8 (dec 2)	A
8	8	A

Tail

Round 1: Using A and MC, work 5 dc. 5 sts

Round 2: Dc around. 10 sts

Round 3: Dc around. 5 sts Break yarn, leaving a long tail.

Round	Stitches	Yarn
1	MC 5	A
2	10 (inc 5)	A
3	5 (dec 5)	A

Making up

Stuff all parts of toy. Attach eyes between rounds 8 and 9, 10 sts across. Embroider mouth. Attach ears, beginning at round 2 of head. Attach limbs and tail. Sew on button.

The Japanese tea ceremony is famous throughout the world, and this set of quirky characters will allow you to stage your own funky version of the celebration.

Chado Tea Set

Materials

Mirasol Hap'i Organic Cotton 100% cotton (120m per 50g)

2 x 50g balls green (A)

1 x 50g ball tan (B)

3.5mm crochet hook

Black embroidery yarn

Toy eyes or black beads

Polyester stuffing

Special techniques

Magic circle (MC)

Double crochet (dc)

Increasing

Decreasing

Size

Teapot: 4in (10cm) high

Cups: 2in (5cm) high

Teapot body

Round 1: Using A and MC, work 8 dc. 8 sts

Round 2: 2dc into each st. 16 sts

Round 3: (2dc in next dc, dc in next dc) rep around. 24 sts

Round 4: (2dc in next dc, dc in next 2 dc) rep around. 32 sts

Round 5: (2dc in next dc, dc in next 3 dc) rep around. 40 sts

Round 6: Dc into each st. 40 sts

Rounds 7–15: Dc around. 40 sts

Round 16: (dc in next 6 dc, dc2tog) rep around. 35 sts

Round 17: Dc around. 35 sts

Round 18: (dc in next 5 dc, dc2tog) rep around. 30 sts

Round 19: (dc in next 4 dc, dc2tog) rep around. 25 sts

Break yarn, leaving a long tail.

Round	Stitches	Yarn
1	MC 8	A
2	16 (inc 8)	A
3	24 (inc 8)	A
4	32 (inc 8)	A
5	40 (inc 8)	A
6	40 sts	A
7–15	40	A
16	35 (dec 5)	A
17	35	A
18	30 (dec 5)	A
19	25 (dec 5)	A

Spout

Round 1: Using A and MC, work 5 dc. 5 sts

Round 2: 2dc into each st. 10 sts

Rounds 3–7: Dc around. 10 sts
Break yarn, leaving a long tail.

Round	Stitches	Yarn
1	MC 5	A
2	10 (inc 5)	A
3–7	10	A

Handle

Round 1: Using B and MC, work 5 dc. 5 sts

Rounds 2–35: Dc around. 5 sts
Break yarn, leaving a long tail.

Round	Stitches	Yarn
1	MC 5	B
2–35	5	B

Tea insert for cup (make 3)

Round 1: Using B and MC, work 6 dc. 6 sts

Round 2: (2dc into each dc) rep around. 12 sts

Round 3: (2dc in next dc, dc in next dc) rep around. 18 sts

Round 4: (2dc in next dc, dc in next 2 dc) rep around. 24 sts

Round 5: Dc around. 24 sts
Break yarn, leaving a long tail.

Round	Stitches	Yarn
1	MC 6	B
2	12 (inc 6)	B
3	18 (inc 6)	B
4	24 (inc 6)	B
5	24	B

Making up

Embroider faces on pot and cups. Stuff toys. Sew 'tea' insert to inside of pot and cups. Attach pot handle.

Tea insert for pot

Round 1: Using B and MC, work 8 dc. 8 sts

Round 2: 2dc into each st. 16 sts

Round 3: (2dc in next dc, dc in next dc) rep around. 24 sts

Round 4: (2dc in next dc, dc in next 2 dc) rep around. 32 sts

Round 5: (2dc in next dc, dc in next 3 dc) rep around. 40 sts

Rounds 6–7: Dc into each st. 40 sts
Break yarn, leaving a long tail.

Round	Stitches	Yarn
1	MC 8	B
2	16 (inc 8)	B
3	24 (inc 8)	B
4	32 (inc 8)	B
5	40 (inc 8)	B
6–7	40	B

Cup (make 3)

Round 1: Using A and MC, work 6 dc. 6 sts

Round 2: (2dc into each dc) rep around. 12 sts

Round 3: (2dc in next dc, dc in next dc) rep around. 18 sts

Round 4: (2dc in next dc, dc in next 2 dc) rep around. 24 sts

Round 5: Dc into each st. 24 sts

Rounds 6–15: Dc around. 24 sts
Break yarn, leaving a long tail.

Round	Stitches	Yarn
1	MC 6	A
2	12 (inc 6)	A
3	18 (inc 6)	A
4	24 (inc 6)	A
5	24	A
6–15	24	A

Some boys may be reluctant to admit that they like cuddly creatures, but this soft toy with a difference should appeal to the bravest and boldest of little men.

Aaron Aeroplane

Materials

Debbie Bliss Cashmerino Chunky 55% merino wool 33% microfibre 12% cashmere (65m per 50g)

1 x 50g ball red (A)

1 x 50g ball blue (B)

Approx 25g white (C)

4mm crochet hook

Polyester stuffing

Embroidery thread

Toy eyes (optional)

Special techniques

Magic circle (MC)

Double crochet (dc)

Increasing

Decreasing

Size

7in (18cm) long

Round 7: Dc around. 32 sts

Change to B.

Round 8: Dc around. 32 sts

Round 9: (2dc in next dc, dc in next 15 dc) rep around. 34 sts

Rounds 10–18: Dc around. 34 sts

Round 19: (dc in next 15 dc, dc2tog) rep around. 32 sts

Round 20: (dc in next 14 dc, dc2tog) rep around. 30 sts

Round 21: (dc in next 13 dc, dc2tog) rep around. 28 sts

Round 22: (dc in next 12 dc, dc2tog) rep around. 26 sts

Round 23: (dc in next 11dc, dc2tog) rep around. 24 sts

Round 24: (dc in next 10 dc, dc2tog) rep around. 22 sts

Round 25: (dc in next 9 dc, dc2tog) rep around. 20 sts

Round 26: (dc in next 8 dc, dc2tog) rep around. 18 sts

Round 27: Dc around. 18 sts

Round 28: (dc in next 7 dc, dc2tog) rep around. 16 sts

Round 29: Dc around. 16 sts

Round 30: (dc in next 6 dc, dc2tog) rep around. 14 sts

Round 31: Dc around. 14 sts

Round 32: (dc in next 5 dc, dc2tog) rep around. 12 sts

Round 33: Dc around. 12 sts

Round 34: (dc2tog) rep around. 6 sts

Round 35: (dc2tog) rep around. 3 sts

Close hole and sew in yarn end.

Round	Stitches	Yarn
1	MC 6	A
2	12 (inc 6)	A
3	18 (inc 6)	A
4	24 (inc 6)	A
5	30 (inc 6)	A
6	32 (inc 2)	A
7	32	A
Change to B		
8	32	B
9	34 (inc 2)	B
10–18	34	B
19	32 (dec 2)	B
20	30 (dec 2)	B
21	28 (dec 2)	B
22	26 (dec 2)	B
23	24 (dec 2)	B
24	22 (dec 2)	B
25	20 (dec 2)	B
26	18 (dec 2)	B
27	18	B
28	16 (dec 2)	B
29	16	B
30	14 (dec 2)	B
31	14	B
32	12 (dec 2)	B
33	12	B
34	6 (dec 6)	B
35	3 (dec 3)	B

Body

Round 1: Using A and MC, work 6 dc. 6 sts

Round 2: 2dc into each st. 12 sts

Round 3: (2dc in next dc, dc in next dc) rep around. 18 sts

Round 4: (2dc in next dc, dc in next 2 dc) rep around. 24 sts

Round 5: (2dc in next dc, dc in next 3 dc) rep around. 30 sts

Round 6: (2dc in next dc, dc in next 14 dc) rep around. 32 sts

Wings (make 2)

Round 1: Using A and MC, work 6 dc. 6 sts

Round 2: 2dc into each st. 12 sts

Round 3: (2dc in next dc, dc in next dc) rep around. 18 sts

Round 4: (2dc in next dc, dc in next 2 dc) rep around. 24 sts

Round 5: (2dc in next dc, dc in next 5 dc) rep around. 28 sts

Rounds 6–8: Dc around. 28 sts
Change to C.

Round 9: Dc around. 28 sts
Change to B.

Rounds 10–11: Dc around. 28 sts
Change to C.

Round 12: Dc around. 28 sts
Change to A.

Round 13: (dc in next 12 dc, dc2tog) rep around. 26 sts

Round 14: (dc in next 11 dc, dc2tog) rep around. 24 sts

Round 15: (dc in next 6 dc, dc2tog) rep around. 18 sts

Rounds 16–18: Dc around. 18 sts
Fasten off, leaving a long tail.
Stuff lightly and sew to side of body.

Round	Stitches	Yarn
1	MC 6	A
2	12 (inc 6)	A
3	18 (inc 6)	A
4	24 (inc 6)	A
5	28 (inc 4)	A
6–8	28	A
Change to C		
9	28	C
Change to B		
10–11	28	B
Change to C		
12	28	C
Change to A		
13	26	A
14	24 (dec 2)	A
15	18 (dec 6)	A
16–18	18	A

Main tailfin

Round 1: Using A and MC, work 6 dc. 6 sts

Round 2: 2dc into each st. 12 sts

Rounds 3–5: Dc around. 12 sts
Break yarn leaving a long tail.
Sew main tailfin to body.

Round	Stitches	Yarn
1	MC 6	A
2	12 (inc 6)	A
3–5	12	A

Side tailfin (make 2)

Round 1: Using C and MC, work 5 dc. 5 sts

Round 2: 2dc into each st. 10 sts

Rounds 3–4: Dc around. 10 sts
Break yarn, leaving a long tail.
Attach to body.

Round	Stitches	Yarn
1	MC 5	C
2	10 (inc 5)	C
3–4	10	C

Cockpit

Round 1: Using C and MC, work 6 dc. 6 sts

Round 2: 2dc into each st. 12 sts

Round 3: (2dc in next dc, dc in next dc) rep around. 18 sts

Rounds 4–5: Dc around. 18 sts
Change to B.

Round 6: Dc around. 18 sts
Break yarn, leaving a long tail.
Sew cockpit to body.

Round	Stitches	Yarn
1	MC 6	C
2	12 (inc 6)	C
3	18 (inc 6)	C
4–5	18	C
Change to B		
6	18	B

Making up

Attach eyes. Make propeller using loops of yarn and attach to nose.

This little character makes the perfect pet:
no mess, no noise, and there's no need to take him for
a walk – unless you want to, that is!

Playful Puppy

Materials

Debbie Bliss Baby Cashmerino 55% merino wool
33% microfibre 12% cashmere (125m per 50g).
1 x 50g ball off-white (A)
10g 204 light blue (B)
3mm crochet hook
Black embroidery yarn
Polyester stuffing
Toy eyes or black beads

Special techniques

Magic circle (MC)
Double crochet (dc)
Increasing
Decreasing

Size

4in (10cm) high

Head

Round 1: Using A and MC, work 5 dc. 5 sts

Round 2: 2dc into each st. 10 sts

Round 3: (2dc in next dc, dc in next dc) rep around. 15 sts

Round 4: (2dc in next dc, dc in next 2 dc) rep around. 20 sts

Round 5: (2dc in next dc, dc in next 3 dc) rep around. 25 sts

Round 6: (2dc in next dc, dc in next 4 dc) rep around. 30 sts

Round 7: (2dc in next dc, dc in next 5 dc) rep around. 35 sts

Rounds 8–10: Dc around. 35 sts

Round 11: (dc in next 5 dc, dc2tog) rep around. 30 sts

Round 12: Dc around. 30 sts

Round 13: (dc in next 4 dc, dc2tog) rep around. 25 sts

Round 14: Dc around. 25 sts

Round 15: (dc in next 3 dc, dc2tog) rep around. 20 sts

Round 16: Dc around. 20 sts

Attach the eyes.

Round 17: (dc in next 2 dc, dc2tog) rep around. 15 sts

Stuff the head.

Round 18: (dc in next dc, dc2tog) rep around. 10 sts

Round 19: (dc2tog) rep around. 5 sts

Round 20: Dc2tog until hole closes. Break yarn, leaving a long tail.

Round	Stitches	Yarn
1	MC 5	A
2	10 (inc 5)	A
3	15 (inc 5)	A
4	20 (inc 5)	A
5	25 (inc 5)	A
6	30 (inc 5)	A
7	35 (inc 5)	A
8–10	35	A
11	30 (dec 5)	A
12	30	A
13	25 (dec 5)	A
14	25	A
15	20 (dec 5)	A
16	20	A
Attach eyes		
17	15 (dec 5)	A
Stuff toy		
18	10 (dec 5)	A
19	5 (dec 5)	A
20	2 into 1	A

Ears (make 2)

Round 1: Using B and MC, work 4 dc. 4 sts

Round 2: 2dc into each st. 8 sts

Round 3: (2dc in next dc, dc in next 3 dc) rep around. 10 sts

Round 4: Dc around. 10 sts

Round 5: (dc in next 3 dc, dc2tog) rep around. 8 sts

Rounds 6–10: Dc around. 8 sts

Break yarn, leaving a long tail.

Attach ears to side of head. Embroider nose, mouth and tongue.

Round	Stitches	Yarn
1	MC 4	B
2	8 (inc 4)	B
3	10 (inc 2)	B
4	10	B
5	8 (dec 2)	B
6–10	8	B

Body

Round 1: Using A and MC, work 5 dc. 5 sts

Round 2: 2dc into each st. 10 sts

Round 3: (2dc in next dc, dc in next dc) rep around. 15 sts

Round 4: (2dc in next dc, dc in next 2 dc) rep around. 20 sts

Round 5: (2dc in next dc, dc in next 3 dc) rep around. 25 sts

Round 6: (2dc in next dc, dc in next 4 dc) rep around. 30 sts

Rounds 7–15: Dc around. 30 sts

Round 16: (2dc in next dc, dc in next 5 dc) rep around. 35 sts

Rounds 17–18: Dc around. 35 sts

Round 19: (dc in next 5 dc, dc2tog) rep around. 30 sts

Round 20: (dc in next 4 dc, dc2tog) rep around. 25 sts

Stuff body.

Round 21: (dc in next 3 dc, dc2tog) rep around. 20 sts

Round 22: (dc in next 2 dc, dc2tog) rep around. 15 sts

Round 23: (dc in next dc, dc2tog) rep around. 10 sts

Round 24: (dc2tog) rep around. 5 sts

Round 25: Dc2tog around until hole closes.

Break yarn, leaving a long tail.

Round	Stitches	Yarn
1	MC 5	A
2	10 (inc 5)	A
3	15 (inc 5)	A
4	20 (inc 5)	A
5	25 (inc 5)	A
6	30 (inc 5)	A
7–15	30	A
16	35 (inc 5)	A
17–18	35	A
19	30 (dec 5)	A
20	25 (dec 5)	A
	Stuff body	
21	20 (dec 5)	A
22	15 (dec 5)	A
23	10 (dec 5)	A
24	5 (dec 5)	A
25	2 into 1	A

Tail

Round 1: Using A and MC, work 5 dc. 5 sts

Rounds 2–10: Dc around. 5 sts

Break yarn, leaving a long tail.

Round	Stitches	Yarn
1	MC 5	A
2–10	10	A

Legs (make 4)

Round 1: Using A and MC, work 4 dc. 4 sts

Round 2: 2dc into each st. 8 sts

Rounds 3–10: Dc around. 8 sts

Break yarn, leaving a long tail.

Round	Stitches	Yarn
1	MC 4	A
2	8 (inc 4)	A
3–10	8	A

Making up

Stuff legs and tail and attach to body.

It's not often that a frog stops hopping for long enough for anyone to get a good look at him – but this amazing amphibian should satisfy the curiosity of any young nature-lover.

Friendly Frog

Materials

Debbie Bliss Cashmerino Aran 55% merino wool
33% microfibre 12% cashmere (90m per 50g)
1 x 50g ball green (A)
10g each of contrast shades B, C and D
3.5mm and 3mm crochet hooks
Black embroidery yarn
Toy eyes or black beads
Stuffing pellets
Small piece of white felt
Fabric adhesive

Special techniques

Magic circle (MC)
Double crochet (dc)
Increasing
Decreasing
Chain stitch (ch)

Size

10in (25cm) tall

Head

Round 1: Using 3.5mm hook, A and MC, work 8 dc. 8 sts

Round 2: 2dc into each st. 16 sts

Round 3: (2dc in next dc, dc in next dc) rep around. 24 sts

Round 4: (2dc in next dc, dc in next 2 dc) rep around. 32 sts

Round 5: (2dc in next dc, dc in next 3 dc) rep around. 40 sts

Round 6: (2dc in next dc, dc in next 4 dc) rep around. 48 sts

Round 7: (2dc in next dc, dc in next 5 dc) rep around. 56 sts

Rounds 8–17: Dc around. 56 sts

Round 18: (dc in next 5 dc, dc2tog) rep around. 48 sts

Round 19: (dc in next 4 dc, dc2tog) rep around. 40 sts

Round 20: (dc in next 3 dc, dc2tog) rep around. 32 sts

Round	Stitches	Yarn
1	MC 8	A
2	16 (inc 8)	A
3	24 (inc 8)	A
4	32 (inc 8)	A
5	40 (inc 8)	A
6	48 (inc 8)	A
7	56 (inc 8)	A
8–17	56	A
18	48 (dec 8)	A
19	40 (dec 8)	A
20	32 (dec 8)	A
21	24 (dec 8)	A

Round 21: (dc in next 2 dc, dc2tog) rep around. 24 sts

Break yarn, leaving a long tail.

Body

Round 1: Using 3mm hook, A and MC, work 8 dc. 8 sts

Round 2: 2dc into each st. 16 sts

Round 3: (2dc in next dc, dc in next dc) rep around. 24 sts

Round 4: (2dc in next dc, dc in next 2 dc) rep around. 32 sts

Round 5: (2dc in next dc, dc in next 3 dc) rep around. 40 sts

Rounds 6–8: Dc around. 40 sts
Change to B.

Round 9: Dc around. 40 sts
Change to C.

Round 10: Dc around. 40 sts
Change to B.

Round 11: (dc2tog) twice, dc rem sts. 38 sts
Change to C.

Round 12: (dc2tog) twice, dc rem sts. 36 sts
Change to B.

Round 13: Dc around. 36 sts
Change to C.

Round 14: (dc2tog) twice, dc rem sts. 34 sts
Change to B.

Round 15: (dc2tog) twice, dc rem sts. 32 sts
Change to C.

Round 16: Dc around. 32 sts
Change to B.

Round 17: (dc2tog) twice, dc rem sts. 30 sts
Change to C.

Round 18: (dc2tog) twice, dc rem sts. 28 sts
Change to B.

Round 19: Dc around. 28 sts
Change to C.

Round 20: (dc2tog) twice, dc rem sts. 26 sts
Change to B.

Round 21: (dc2tog) twice, dc rem sts. 24 sts

Break yarn, leaving a long tail.

Round	Stitches	Yarn
1	MC 8	A
2	16 (inc 8)	A
3	24 (inc 8)	A
4	32 (inc 8)	A
5	40 (inc 8)	A
6–8	40	A
Begin contrast stripes		
9	40	B
10	40	C
11	38 (dec 2)	B
12	36 (dec 2)	C
13	36	B
14	34 (dec 2)	C
15	32 (dec 2)	B
16	32	C
17	30 (dec 2)	B
18	28 (dec 2)	C
19	28	B
20	26 (dec 2)	C
21	24 (dec 2)	B

Arms and legs

Round 1: Using 3mm hook, A and MC, work 8 dc. 8 sts

Round 2: 2dc into each dc. 16 sts

Round 3: Dc around. 16 sts

Round 4: Dc2tog around. 8 sts

Rounds 5–15: Dc around. 8 sts

Break yarn, leaving a long tail.

Round	Stitches	Yarn
1	MC 8	A
2	16 (inc 8)	A
3	16	A
4	8 (dec 8)	A
5–15	8	A

Eye pieces

Round 1: Using 3mm hook, A and MC, work 7 dc. 7 sts

Round 2: 2dc into each st. 14 sts

Round 3: (2dc in next dc, dc in next 6 dc) rep around. 16 sts

Rounds 4–7: Dc around. 16 sts

Round 8: (dc2tog, dc in next 6 dc) rep around. 14 sts

Break yarn, leaving a long tail.

Round	Stitches	Yarn
1	MC 7	A
2	14 (inc 7)	A
3	16 (inc 2)	A
4–7	16	A
8	14 (dec 2)	A

Scarf

Round 1: Using 3mm hook and D, work 65ch.

Round 2: 1dc into each ch. 65 sts

Break yarn and sew in tail.

Making up

Cut two felt semi-circles slightly smaller than the eyes. Sew to eye pieces, beg one round from bottom. Insert eyes, piercing a small hole in the felt first if necessary. Stuff eye pieces and attach to head, beg at round 3. Embroider mouth. Stuff head, body and limbs and attach head and limbs to body.

This gorgeous toy would be an ideal bedtime companion
for any little girl: something soft and cuddly to hug while she has
sweet dreams of growing up to be a famous dancer.

Ballerina Bunny

Materials

Debbie Bliss Cotton DK 100% cotton (84m per 50g)

1 x 50g ball pale pink (A)

1 x 50g ball cream (B)

1 x 50g ball bright pink (C)

3.5mm crochet hook

Oddments of pink and black yarn for face

Safety eyes

Polyester toy filling

Special techniques

Magic circle (MC)

Double crochet (dc)

Increasing

Decreasing

Size

11in (28cm) tall

Ears (make 2)

Round 1: Using A and MC, work 7 dc. 7 sts

Round 2: 2dc into each dc. 14 sts

Rounds 3–8: Dc around. 14 sts

Round 9: Dc2tog, dc rem sts. 13 sts

Round 10: Dc around. 13 sts

Round 11: Dc2tog, dc rem sts. 12 sts

Round 12: Dc around. 12 sts

Round 13: Dc2tog, dc rem sts. 11 sts

Round 14: Dc around. 11 sts

Break yarn, leaving a long tail.

Round	Stitches	Yarn
1	MC 7	A
2	14 (inc 7)	A
3–8	14	A
9	13 (dec 1)	A
10	13	A
11	12 (dec 1)	A
12	12	A
13	11 (dec 1)	A
14	11	A

Head

Round 1: Using B and MC, work 8 dc. 8 sts

Round 2: 2dc into each st. 16 sts

Round 3: (2dc in next dc, dc in next dc) rep around. 24 sts

Round 4: (2dc in next dc, dc in next 2 dc) rep around. 32 sts

Round 5: (2dc in next dc, dc in next 3 dc) rep around. 40 sts

Round 6: (2dc in next dc, dc in next 4 dc) rep around. 48 sts

Round 7: *(2dc in next dc, dc in next 10 dc) rep from * 4 times, dc last 4 sts. 52 sts

Rounds 8–18: Dc around. 52 sts.

Round 19: *(dc in next 10dc, dc2tog) rep from * 4 times, dc last 4 sts. 48 sts

Round 20: (dc in next 4 dc, dc2tog) rep around. 40 sts

Round 21: (dc in next 3 dc, dc2tog) rep around. 32 sts

Round 22: (dc in next 2 dc, dc2tog) rep around. 24 sts

Break yarn, leaving a long tail.

Round	Stitches	Yarn
1	MC 8	B
2	16 (inc 8)	B
3	24 (inc 8)	B
4	32 (inc 8)	B
5	40 (inc 8)	B
6	48 (inc 8)	B
7	52 (inc 4)	B
8–18	52	B
19	48 (dec 4)	B
20	40 (dec 8)	B
21	32 (dec 8)	B
22	24 (dec 8)	B

Body

Alternate A and C every 2 rounds.

Round 1: Using A and MC, work 8 dc. 8 sts

Round 2: 2dc into each dc. 16 sts

Round 3: (2dc in next dc, dc in next dc) rep around. 24 sts

Round 4: (2dc in next dc, dc in next 2 dc) rep around. 32 sts

Round 5: (2dc in next dc, dc in next 3 dc) rep around. 40 sts

Round 6: (2dc in next dc, dc in next 4 dc) rep around. 48 sts

Rounds 7–18: Dc around. 48 sts

Round 19: (dc in next 4 dc, dc2tog) rep around. 40 sts

Round 20: Dc around. 40 sts

Round 21: (dc in next 3 dc, dc2tog) rep around. 32 sts

Round 22: Dc around. 32 sts

Round 23: (dc in next 2 dc, dc2tog) rep around. 24 sts

Round 24: Dc around. 24 sts

Rounds 25–26: Dc around. 24 sts

Break yarn, leaving a long tail.

Round	Stitches	Yarn
1	MC 8	A
2	16 (inc 8)	A
3	24 (inc 8)	C
4	32 (inc 8)	C
5	40 (inc 8)	A
6	48 (inc 8)	A
7–18	48	alt C and A
19	40 (dec 8)	C
20	40	C
21	32 (dec 8)	A
22	32	A
23	24 (dec 8)	C
24	24	C
25–26	24	A

Arms (make 2)

Round 1: Using B and MC, work 6 dc. 6 sts

Round 2: 2dc into each st. 12 sts

Rounds 3–5: Dc around. 12 sts

Round 6: (dc in next 2 dc, dc2tog) rep around. 9 sts

Rounds 7–11: Dc around. 9 sts Change to C.

Rounds 12–13: Dc around. 9 sts Change to A.

Rounds 14–15: Dc around. 9 sts Break yarn, leaving a long tail.

Round	Stitches	Yarn
1	MC 6	B
2	12 (inc 6)	B
3–5	12	B
6	9 (dec 3)	B
7–11	9	B
12–13	9	C
14–15	9	A

Legs (make 2)

Round 1: Using C and MC, work 7 dc. 7 sts

Round 2: 2dc into each st. 14 sts.

Round 3: 2dc into the first st, dc into rem sts. 15 sts

Rounds 4–7: Dc around. 15 sts Change to B.

Round 8: (dc in next 3 dc, dc2tog) rep around. 12 sts

Rounds 9–12: Dc around. 12 sts Break yarn, leaving a long tail.

Round	Stitches	Yarn
1	MC 7	C
2	14 (inc 7)	C
3	15 (inc 1)	C
4–7	15	C
8	12 (dec 3)	B
9–12	12	B

Skirt (make 1)

Round 1: Using C, work 48ch and sl st to join.

Round 2: 2dc into each st. 96 sts

Round 3: 3dc into each st. 288 sts Break yarn, leaving a long tail.

Making up

Attach eyes between rounds 12 and 13, 10 sts apart. Stuff toy parts and attach head and limbs to body. Sew skirt to body at round 14 from beg of magic circle. Attach ears, beg at round 2. Embroider nose and mouth.

This little creature might look cross, but in reality he's as cuddly as a teddy bear. He's ideal for any little boy who secretly likes soft toys but wants something a bit more macho to play with.

Disgruntled Dino

Materials

100g Debbie Bliss Rialto Aran 100% merino wool
(80m per 50g)
1 × 50g ball aqua (A)
1 × 50g ball lemon (B)
1 × 50g ball blue (C)
3.5mm crochet hook
Black embroidery yarn
Polyester stuffing
Safety eyes or black beads

Special techniques

Magic circle (MC)
Double crochet (dc)
Increasing
Decreasing

Size

8in (20cm) tall

Head

Round 1: Using 3.5mm hook, A and MC, work 6 dc. 6 sts

Round 2: 2dc into each st. 12 sts

Round 3: (2dc in next dc, dc in next dc) rep around. 18 sts

Round 4: (2dc in next dc, dc in next 2 dc) rep around. 24 sts

Round 5: (2dc in next dc, dc in next 3 dc) rep around. 30 sts

Round 6: (2dc in next dc, dc in next 4 dc) rep around. 36 sts

Round 7: (2dc in next dc, dc in next 5 dc) rep around. 42 sts

Rounds 8–20: Dc around. 42 sts

Round 21: (dc in next 5dc, dc2tog) rep around. 36 sts

Round 22: (dc in next 4dc, dc2tog) rep around. 30 sts

Attach eyes, embroider mouth, stuff.

Round 23: (dc in next 3dc, dc2tog) rep around. 24 sts

Round 24: (dc in next 2dc, dc2tog) rep around. 18 sts

Round 25: (dc in next dc, dc2tog) rep around. 12 sts

Round 26: (dc2tog) rep around. 6 sts
Work 2 sts into 1 until hole closes.
Fasten off and sew in yarn tail.

Round	Stitches	Yarn
1	MC 6	A
2	12 (inc 6)	A
3	18 (inc 6)	A
4	24 (inc 6)	A
5	30 (inc 6)	A
6	36 (inc 6)	A
7	42 (inc 6)	A
8–20	42	A
21	36 (dec 6)	A
22	30 (dec 6)	A
Attach eyes, embroider mouth and nose. Stuff.		
23	24 (dec 6)	A
24	18 (dec 6)	A
25	12 (dec 6)	A
26	6 (dec 6)	A

Body

Round 1: Using A and MC, work 6 dc. 6 sts

Round 2: 2dc into each st. 12 sts

Round 3: (2dc in next dc, dc in next dc) rep around. 18 sts

Round 4: (2dc in next dc, dc in next 2 dc) rep around. 24 sts

Round 5: (2dc in next dc, dc in next 3 dc) rep around. 30 sts

Round 6: (2dc in next dc, dc in next 4 dc) rep around. 36 sts

Round 7: (2dc in next dc, dc in next 5 dc) rep around. 42 sts

Rounds 8–19: Dc around. 42 sts
Change to B.

Rounds 20–25: Dc around. 42 sts

Round 26: (dc in next 5 dc, dc2tog) rep around. 36 sts

Rounds 27–28: Dc around. 36 sts

Round 29: (dc in next 4 dc, dc2tog) rep around. 30 sts

Rounds 30–31: Dc around. 30 sts
Change to A.

Round 32: Dc around. 30 sts
Break yarn, leaving a long tail.
Stuff body and sew to head.

Round	Stitches	Yarn
1	MC 6	A
2	12 (inc 6)	A
3	18 (inc 6)	A
4	24 (inc 6)	A
5	30 (inc 6)	A
6	36 (inc 6)	A
7	42 (inc 6)	A
8–19	42	A
20–25	42	B
26	36 (dec 6)	B
27–28	36	B
29	30 (dec 6)	B
30–31	30	B
32	30	A

Tail

Round 1: Using A and MC, work 4 dc. 4 sts

Round 2: 2dc into each st. 8 sts

Round 3: Dc around. 8 sts

Round 4: (2dc in next dc, dc in next dc) rep around. 12 sts

Round 5: Dc around. 12 sts

Round 6: (2dc in next dc, dc in next 2 dc) rep around. 16 sts

Rounds 7–8: Dc around. 16 sts

Round 9: (2dc in next dc, dc in next 7 dc) rep around. 18 sts

Rounds 10–11: Dc around. 18 sts

Round 12: (2dc in next dc, dc in next 8 dc) rep around. 20 sts

Round 13–14: Dc around. 20 sts

Round 15: (2dc in next dc, dc in next 9 dc) rep around. 22 sts

Rounds 16–17: Dc around. 22 sts

Round 18: (2dc in next dc, dc in next 10 dc) rep around. 24 sts

Rounds 19–20: Dc around. 24 sts

Round 21: (2dc in next dc, dc in next 11 dc) rep around. 26 sts

Round 22: (2dc in next dc, dc in next 12 dc) rep around. 28 sts

Round 23: (2dc in next dc, dc in next 13 dc) rep around. 30 sts

Round 24: (2dc in next dc, dc in next 14 dc) rep around. 32 sts

Round 25: (2dc in next dc, dc in next 15 dc) rep around. 34 sts

Round 26: (2dc in next dc, dc in next 16 dc) rep around. 36 sts

Break yarn, leaving a long tail. Stuff tail and sew to body.

Round	Stitches	Yarn
1	MC 4	A
2	8 (inc 4)	A
3	8	A
4	12 (inc 4)	A
5	12	A
6	16 (inc 4)	A
7–8	16	A
9	18 (inc 2)	A
10–11	18	A
12	20 (inc 2)	A
13–14	20	A
15	22 (inc 2)	A
16–17	22	A
18	24 (inc 2)	A
19–20	24	A
21	26 (inc 2)	A
22	28 (inc 2)	A
23	30 (inc 2)	A
24	32 (inc 2)	A
25	34 (inc 2)	A
26	36 (inc 2)	A

Spikes (make 7)

Round 1: Using C and MC, work 4 dc. 4 sts

Round 2: 2dc into each dc. 8 sts

Round 3: (2dc in next dc, dc in next dc) rep around. 12 sts

Rounds 4–6: Dc around. 12 sts

Break yarn, leaving a long tail.

Attach spikes, evenly spaced, down head, body and tail.

Round	Stitches	Yarn
1	MC 4	C
2	8 (inc 4)	C
3	12 (inc 4)	C
4–6	12	C

Arms (make 2)

Round 1: Using A and MC, work 5 dc. 5 sts

Round 2: 2dc into each st. 10 sts

Rounds 3–9: Dc around. 10 sts
Change to C.

Rounds 10–11: Dc around. 10 sts
Break yarn, leaving a long tail. Stuff arms. Using black thread and blanket stitch, work fingers. Sew hole to close. Attach arms to body.

Round	Stitches	Yarn
1	MC 5	A
2	10 (inc 5)	A
3–9	10	A
10–11	10	C

Legs (make 2)

Round 1: Using A and MC, work 6 dc. 6 sts

Round 2: 2dc into each st. 12 sts

Round 3: (2dc in next dc, dc in next dc) rep around. 18 sts

Round 4: (2dc in next dc, dc in next 2 dc) rep around. 24 sts

Rounds 5–7: Dc around. 24 sts

Round 8: (dc in next 10 dc, dc2tog) rep around. 22 sts

Round 9: (dc in next 9 dc, dc2tog) rep around. 20 sts

Round 10: (dc in next 8 dc, dc2tog) rep around. 18 sts

Round 11: (dc in next 2 dc, dc2tog) rep around. 12 sts

Rounds 12–14: Dc around. 12 sts
Change to C.

Rounds 15–16: Dc around. 12 sts
Stuff leg.

Round 17: (dc2tog) rep around. 6 sts
Break yarn, leaving a long tail. Using black, work blanket stitch to form toes. Close hole. Attach legs to body.

Round	Stitches	Yarn
1	MC 6	A
2	12 (inc 6)	A
3	18 (inc 6)	A
4	24 (inc 6)	A
5–7	24	A
8	22 (dec 2)	A
9	20 (dec 2)	A
10	18 (dec 2)	A
11	12 (dec 6)	A
12–14	12	A
Change to C		
15–16	12	C
Stuff		
17	6 (dec 6)	C

These fascinating birds are always among
the most popular of cuddly toys. Why not make a few, and stage
your own march of the penguins?

Percy Penguin

Materials

Debbie Bliss Cashmerino Aran 55% merino wool
33% microfibre 12% cashmere (90m per 50g)
1 × 50g ball black (A)
25g yellow (B)
3.5mm crochet hook
Toy eyes
Polyester stuffing
Piece of white felt or fabric

Special techniques

Magic circle (MC)
Double crochet (dc)
Increasing
Decreasing

Size

5in (13cm) tall

Round	Stitches	Yarn
1	MC 5	A
2	10 (inc 5)	A
3	15 (inc 5)	A
4	20 (inc 5)	A
5	25 (inc 5)	A
6	30 (inc 5)	A
7	30	A
8	35 (inc 5)	A
9–10	35	A
11	36 (inc 1)	A
12	36	A
13	37 (inc 1)	A
14	37	A

Head

Round 1: Using A and MC, work 5 dc. 5 sts

Round 2: 2dc into each st. 10 sts

Round 3: (2dc in next dc, dc in next dc) rep around. 15 sts

Round 4: (2dc in next dc, dc in next 2 dc) rep around. 20 sts

Round 5: (2dc in next dc, dc in next 3 dc) rep around. 25 sts

Round 6: (2dc in next dc, dc in next 4 dc) rep around. 30 sts

Round 7: Dc around. 30 sts

Round 8: (2dc in next dc, dc in next 5 dc) rep around. 35 sts

Rounds 9–10: Dc around. 35 sts

Round 11: 2dc in next dc, dc rem sts. 36 sts

Round 12: Dc around. 35 sts

Round 13: 2dc in next dc, dc rem sts. 37 sts

Round 14: Dc around. 37 sts
Break yarn, leaving a long tail.

Beak (make 1)

Round 1: Using C and MC, work 7 dc. 7 sts

Round 2: 2dc into each st. 14 sts

Round 3: (2dc in next dc, dc in next 6 dc) rep around. 16 sts

Rounds 4–6: Dc around. 16 sts
Break yarn, leaving a long tail.

Round	Stitches	Yarn
1	MC 7	B
2	14 (inc 7)	B
3	16 (inc 2)	B
4–6	16	B

Body

Round 1: Using A and MC, work 5 dc. 5 sts

Round 2: 2dc into each dc. 10 sts

Round 3: (2dc in next dc, dc in next dc) rep around. 15 sts

Round 4: (2dc in next dc, dc in next 2 dc) rep around. 20 sts

Round 5: (2dc in next dc, dc in next 3 dc) rep around. 25 sts

Round 6: (2dc in next dc, dc in next 4 dc) rep around. 30 sts

Round 7: (2dc in next dc, dc in next 5 dc) rep around. 35 sts

Round 8: (2dc in next dc, dc in next 6 dc) rep around. 40 sts

Rounds 9–18: Dc around. 40 sts

Round 19: 2dc in next dc, dc in next 18 dc, dc rem sts. 38 sts

Round 20: Dc around. 38 sts

Round 21: 2dc in next dc, dc rem sts. 37 sts

Round 22: Dc around. 37 sts
Break yarn and sew in tail.
Stuff head and body. Stuff beak and sew on. Attach safety eyes. Join head to body. Cut felt oval and sew to front.

Round	Stitches	Yarn
1	MC 5	A
2	10 (inc 5)	A
3	15 (inc 5)	A
4	20 (inc 5)	A
5	25 (inc 5)	A
6	30 (inc 5)	A
7	35 (inc 5)	A
8	40 (inc 5)	A
9–18	40	A
19	38 (dec 2)	A
20	38	A
21	37 (dec 1)	A
22	37	A

Wings (make 2)

Round 1: Using MC, work 6 dc. 6 sts

Round 2: 2dc into each st. 12 sts

Round 3: (2dc in next dc, dc in next dc) rep around. 18 sts

Round 4: (2dc in next dc, dc in next 2 dc) rep around. 24 sts

Round 5: Dc around. 24 sts

Round 6: (2dc in next dc, dc in next 11 dc) rep around. 26 sts

Round 7: Dc around. 26 sts

Round 8: (dc in next 11 dc, dc2tog) rep around. 24 sts

Round 9: Dc around. 24 sts

Round 10: (dc in next 10dc, dc2tog) rep around. 22 sts

Round 11: Dc around. 22 sts

Round 12: (dc in next 9 dc, dc2tog) rep around. 20 sts

Round 13: Dc around. 20 sts

Round 14: (dc in next 8 dc, dc2tog) rep around. 18 sts

Round 15: Dc around. 18 sts

Round 16: (dc in next 7 dc, dc2tog) rep around. 16 sts

Break yarn, leaving a long tail.

Sew wings to body.

Round	Stitches	Yarn
1	MC 6	A
2	12 (inc 6)	A
3	18 (inc 6)	A
4	24 (inc 6)	A
5	24	A
6	26 (inc 2)	A
7	26	A
8	24 (dec 2)	A
9	24	A
10	22 (dec 2)	A
11	22	A
12	20 (dec 2)	A
13	20	A
14	18 (dec 2)	A
15	18	A
16	16 (dec 2)	A

Feet (make 2)

Round 1: Using B and MC, work 5 dc. 5 sts

Round 2: 2dc into each dc. 10 sts

Round 3: (2dc in next dc, dc in next dc) rep around. 15 sts

Round 4: (2dc in next dc, dc in next 2 dc) rep around. 20 sts

Round 5: Dc around. 20 sts

Round 6: (dc in next 2 dc, dc2tog) rep around. 15 sts

Round 7: (dc in next dc, dc2tog) rep around. 10 sts

Rounds 8–10: Dc around. 10 sts

Break yarn, leaving a long tail.

Sew feet to body.

Round	Stitches	Yarn
1	MC 5	B
2	10 (inc 5)	B
3	15 (inc 5)	B
4	20 (inc 5)	B
5	20	B
6	15 (dec 5)	B
7	10 (dec 5)	B
8–10	10	B

Here's another one for the boys!
This mechanical marvel substitutes soft yarn for hard metal for
a toy that is much kinder to the family's furniture.

Robbo Robot

Materials

Debbie Bliss Eco Cotton 100% cotton (50m per 50g)

2 x 50g balls grey (A)

1 x 50g ball red (B)

1 x 50g ball turquoise (C)

3.5mm crochet hook

Polyester toy filling

Safety eyes

Black embroidery thread

Special techniques

Magic circle (MC)

Double crochet (dc)

Increasing

Decreasing

Size

10in (26cm) tall

Head (make 1)

Round 1: Using A and MC, work 7 dc. 7 sts

Round 2: 2dc into each st. 14 sts

Round 3: (2dc in next dc, dc in next dc) rep around. 21 sts

Round 4: (2dc in next dc, dc in next 2 dc) rep around. 28 sts

Round 5: (2dc in next dc, dc in next 3 dc) rep around. 35 sts

Round 6: (2dc in next dc, dc in next 4 dc) rep around. 42 sts

Round 7: (2dc in next dc, dc in next 5 dc) rep around. 49 sts

Round 8: (2dc in next dc, dc in next 6 dc) rep around. 56 sts

Rounds 9–18: Dc around. 56 sts

Round 19: (dc in next 6 dc, dc2tog) rep around. 49 sts

Round 20: (dc in next 2 dc, dc2tog) rep around. 37 sts

Round 21: *(dc in next dc, dc2tog) rep from * to last st, dc last st. 25 sts
Break yarn, leaving a long tail.

Round	Stitches	Yarn
1	MC 7	A
2	14 (inc 7)	A
3	21 (inc 7)	A
4	28 (inc 7)	A
5	35 (inc 7)	A
6	42 (inc 7)	A
7	49 (inc 7)	A
8	56 (inc 7)	A
9–18	56	A
19	49 (dec 7)	A
20	37 (dec 12)	A
21	25	A

Body (make 1)

Round 1: Using A and MC, work 7 dc. 7 sts

Round 2: 2dc into each st. 14 sts

Round 3: (2dc in next dc, dc in next dc) rep around. 21 sts

Round 4: (2dc in next dc, dc in next 2 dc) rep around. 28 sts

Round 5: (2dc in next dc, dc in next 3 dc) rep around. 35 sts

Round 6: (2dc in next dc, dc in next 4 dc) rep around. 42 sts

Round 7: (2dc in next dc, dc in next 5 dc) rep around. 49 sts

Round 8: (2dc in next dc, dc in next 6 dc) rep around. 56 sts

Round 9: *(dc in next 11 dc, 2dc in next dc) rep from * to last 8 sts, work 8 dc. 60 sts

Rounds 10–15: Dc around. 60 sts
Change to C.

Round 16: Dc around. 60 sts.
Change to B.

Round 17: Dc around. 60 sts
Change to C.

Round 18: Dc around. 60 sts
Change to A.

Rounds 19–24: Dc around. 60 sts

Round 25: *(dc in next 9 dc, dc2tog) rep from * to last 5 sts, work 5dc. 55 sts

Rounds 26–27: Dc around. 55 sts

Round 28: (dc in next 3 dc, dc2tog) rep around. 44 sts

Round 29: Dc around. 44 sts

Round 30: *(dc in next 2 dc, dc2tog) rep around. 33 sts

Round 31: (dc in next dc, dc2tog) rep around. 22 sts

Round	Stitches	Yarn
1	MC 7	A
2	14 (inc 7)	A
3	21 (inc 7)	A
4	28 (inc 7)	A
5	35 (inc 7)	A
6	42 (inc 7)	A
7	49 (inc 7)	A
8	56 (inc 6)	A
9	60 (inc 4)	A
10–15	60	A
16	60	C
17	60	B
18	60	C
19–24	60	A
25	55 (dec 5)	A
26–27	55	A
28	44 (dec 11)	A
29	44	A
30	33 (dec 11)	A
31	22 (dec 11)	A

Ears (make 2)

Round 1: Using B and MC, work 7 dc. 7 sts

Round 2: 2dc into each st. 14 sts
Change to A.

Round 3: (2dc in next dc, dc in next dc) rep around. 21 sts

Round 4: Dc around. 21 sts

Round 5: *(dc in next 4 dc, dc2tog) rep from * 3 times, dc into last 3 dc. 18 sts

Rounds 6–7: Dc around. 18 sts
Break yarn, leaving a long tail.

Round	Stitches	Yarn
1	MC 7	B
2	14 (inc 7)	B
	change to A	
3	21 (inc 7)	A
4	21	A
5	18 (dec 3)	A
6–7	18	A

Arm (make 2)

Round 1: Using C and MC, work 5 dc. 5 sts

Round 2: 2dc into each st. 10 sts

Round 3: (2dc in next dc, dc in next dc) rep around. 15 sts

Round 4: Dc around. 15 sts

Round 5: *(dc in next dc, dc2tog) rep from * 5 times. 10 sts

Round 6: *(dc in next 3 dc, dc2tog) rep from * twice. 8 sts
Now work alt rounds A and C, beg A.

Rounds 7–20: Dc around. 8 sts
Break yarn, leaving a long tail.

Round	Stitches	Yarn
1	MC 5	C
2	10 (inc 5)	C
3	15 (inc 5)	C
4	15	C
5	10 (dec 5)	C
6	8 (dec 2)	C
7–20	8	alt A and C

Legs (make 2)

Round 1: Using B and MC, work 7 dc. 7 sts

Round 2: 2dc into each st. 14 sts

Round 3: (2dc in next dc, dc in next dc) rep around. 21 sts

Round 4: (2dc in next dc, dc in next 2 dc) rep around. 28 sts

Rounds 5–7: Dc around. 28 sts

Round 8: (dc in next 2 dc, dc2tog) rep around. 21 sts

Round 9: (dc in next 5 dc, dc2tog) rep around. 18 sts

Round 10: (dc in next 4 dc, dc2tog) rep around. 15 sts
Beg A, work alt rounds A and B.

Round 11: *(dc in next 5 dc, dc2tog) rep from * twice, dc rem st. 13 sts

Rounds 12–20: Dc around. 13 sts
Break yarn, leaving a long tail.

Round	Stitches	Yarn
1	MC 7	B
2	14 (inc 7)	B
3	21 (inc 7)	B
4	28 (inc 7)	B
5–7	28	B
8	21 (dec 7)	B
9	18 (dec 3)	B
10	15 (dec 3)	B
11	13 (dec 2)	A
12–20	13	alt A and B

Making up

Attach ears to opposite sides of head, 10 rounds from top. Attach eyes between rounds 11 and 12. Embroider mouth. Sew head to body. Attach arms, 2 rounds from where head joins body. Attach legs.

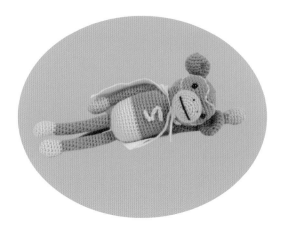

Is it a baboon? Is it an orang-utang? No, it's Supermonkey!
This brave chap is sure to come to the rescue of all your toys
with a flourish of his dashing cape.

Supermonkey

Materials

Debbie Bliss Cashmerino Aran 55% merino wool
33% microfibre 12% cashmere (90m per 50g ball)
100g brown (A)
50g beige (B)
50g yellow (C)
3mm and 3.5mm crochet hooks
Black embroidery yarn
Toy eyes or black beads
Polyester stuffing
Square of felt or fabric for cape

Special techniques

Magic circle (MC)
Double crochet (dc)
Increasing
Decreasing

Size

10in (26cm) tall

Head

Round 1: Using 3.5mm hook, A and MC, work 6 dc. 6 sts

Round 2: 2dc into each st. 12 sts

Round 3: (2dc in next dc, dc in next dc) rep around. 18 sts

Round 4: (2dc in next dc, dc in next 2 dc) rep around. 24 sts

Round 5: (2dc in next dc, dc in next 3 dc) rep around. 30 sts

Round 6: (2dc in next dc, dc in next 4 dc) rep around. 36 sts

Round 7: (2dc in next dc, dc in next 5 dc) rep around. 42 sts

Rounds 8–15: Dc around. 42 sts

Round 16: (dc in next 5 dc, dc2tog) rep around. 36 sts

Round 17: (dc in next 4 dc, dc2tog) rep around. 30 sts

Round 18: (dc in next 3 dc, dc2tog) rep around. 24 sts

Round 19: (dc in next 7 dc, dc2tog) rep around. 20 sts

Break yarn, leaving a long tail.

Round	Stitches	Yarn
1	MC 6	A
2	12 (inc 6)	A
3	18 (inc 6)	A
4	24 (inc 6)	A
5	30 (inc 6)	A
6	36 (inc 6)	A
7	42 (inc 6)	A
8–15	42	A
16	36 (dec 6)	A
17	30 (dec 6)	A
18	24 (dec 6)	A
19	20 (dec 4)	A

Ears

Round 1: Using 3.5mm hook, A and MC, work 5 dc. 5 sts

Round 2: 2dc into each st. 10 sts

Round 3: (2dc in next dc, dc in next dc) rep around. 15 sts

Round 4: (2dc in next dc, dc in next 2 dc) rep around. 20 sts

Rounds 5–6: Dc around. 20 sts

Round 7: (dc in next 2 dc, dc2tog) rep around. 15 sts

Round 8: (dc in next dc, dc2tog) rep around. 10 sts

Break yarn, leaving a long tail.

Round	Stitches	Yarn
1	MC 5	A
2	10 (inc 5)	A
3	15 (inc 5)	A
4	20 (inc 5)	A
5–6	20	A
7	15 (dec 5)	A
8	10 (dec 5)	A

Muzzle

Round 1: Using 3.5mm hook, B and MC, work 5 dc. 5 sts

Round 2: 2dc into each st. 10 sts

Round 3: (2dc in next dc, dc in next dc) rep around. 15 sts

Round 4: (2dc in next dc, dc in next 2 dc) rep around. 20 sts

Round 5: (2dc in next dc, dc in next 3 dc) rep around. 25 sts

Rounds 6–8: Dc around. 25 sts

Round 9: (dc in next 3 dc, dc2tog) rep around. 20 sts

Break yarn, leaving a long tail.

Round	Stitches	Yarn
1	MC 5	B
2	10 (inc 5)	B
3	15 (inc 5)	B
4	20 (inc 5)	B
5	25 (inc 5)	B
6–8	25	B
9	20 (dec 5)	B

Body

Round 1: Using 3.5mm hook, C and MC, work 6 dc. 6 sts

Round 2: 2dc into each st. 12 sts

Round 3: (2dc in next dc, dc in next dc) rep around. 18 sts

Round 4: (2dc in next dc, dc in next 2 dc) rep around. 24 sts

Round 5: (2dc in next dc, dc in next 3 dc) rep around. 30 sts

Round 6: (2dc in next dc, dc in next 4 dc) rep around. 36 sts

Rounds 7–11: Dc around. 36 sts
Change to A.

Rounds 12–21: Dc around. 36 sts

Round 22: (dc in next 4dc, dc2tog) rep around. 30 sts

Round 23: (dc in next 3dc, dc2tog) rep around. 24 sts

Round 24: (dc in next 2dc, dc2tog) rep around. 18 sts

Break yarn, leaving a long tail.

Round	Stitches	Yarn
1	MC 6	C
2	12 (inc 6)	C
3	18 (inc 6)	C
4	24 (inc 6)	C
5	30 (inc 6)	C
6	36 (inc 6)	C
7–11	36	C
Change to A		
12–21	36	A
22	30 (dec 6)	A
23	24 (dec 6)	A
24	18 (dec 6)	A

Arms (make 2)

Round 1: Using 3.5mm hook, B and M, work 5 dc. 5 sts

Round 2: 2dc into each st. 10 sts

Round 3: (2dc in next dc, dc in next 4 dc) rep around. 12 sts

Rounds 4–6: Dc around. 12 sts

Round 7: (dc in next 4 dc, dc2tog) rep around. 10 sts

Round 8: (dc in next 3 dc, dc2tog) rep around. 8 sts
Change to A.

Rounds 9–25: Dc around. 8 sts
Break yarn, leaving a long tail.

Round	Stitches	Yarn
1	MC 5	B
2	10 (inc 5)	B
3	12 (inc 2)	B
4–6	12	B
7	10 (dec 2)	B
8	8 (dec 2)	B
Change to A		
9–25	8	A

Legs (make 2)

Round 1: Using 3.5mm hook, C and MC, work 5dc. 5 sts

Round 2: 2dc into each st. 10 sts

Round 3: (2dc in next dc, dc in next 4 dc) rep around. 12 sts

Rounds 4–6: Dc around. 12 sts

Round 7: (dc in next 4 dc, dc2tog) rep around. 10 sts

Round 8: (dc in next 3 dc, dc2tog) rep around. 8 sts
Change to A.

Rounds 9–25: Dc around. 8 sts
Break yarn, leaving a long tail.

Round	Stitches	Yarn
1	MC 5	C
2	10 (inc 5)	C
3	12 (inc 2)	C
4–6	12	C
7	10 (dec 2)	C
8	8 (dec 2)	C
Change to A		
9–25	8	A

Tail

Round 1: Using 3mm hook, A and MC, work 5 dc. 5 sts

Rounds 2–25: Dc around. 5 sts
Break yarn. leaving a long tail.

Round	Stitches	Yarn
1	MC 5	A
2–25	5	A

Initial trim

Using C, make 16ch and attach neatly to body to form an 'S' shape.

Making up

Stuff all parts. Stuff muzzle lightly and sew to head. Attach eyes. Embroider mouth and face markings. Attach ears. Sew head, limbs and tail to body. Tie or sew fabric square round neck to form the cape, gathering slightly.

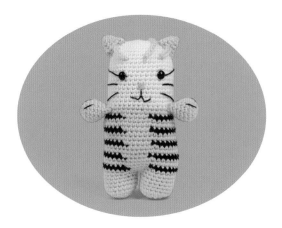

Big cats are usually fierce, but this tiny feline is really friendly. He's perfect for little fingers to hold, and would make an ideal first toy for a baby.

Timmy Tiger

Materials

Debbie Bliss Cashmerino Aran 55% merino wool
33% microfibre 12% cashmere (90m per 50g)
1 x 50g ball yellow (A)
Approx 25g black (B)
Approx 25g white (C)
3.5mm crochet hook
Polyester stuffing
Pink and black embroidery yarn
Safety eyes

Special techniques

Magic circle (MC)
Double crochet (dc)
Increasing
Decreasing
Chain stitch (ch)

Size

7in (18cm) tall

Head and body

Round 1: Using C and MC, work 7 dc. 7 sts

Round 2: 2dc into each st. 14 sts

Round 3: (2dc in next dc, dc in next dc) rep around. 21 sts

Round 4: (2dc in next dc, dc in next 2 dc) rep around. 28 sts

Round 5: (2dc in next dc, dc in next 3 dc) rep around. 35 sts

Round 6: (2dc in next dc, dc in next 14 dc) rep around. 42 sts

Rounds 7–20: Dc around. 42 sts
Change to A.

Rounds 21–22: Dc around. 42 sts
Now use B and A along same round, carrying yarn not in use across back.

Round 23: Dc18B, 6A, 18B. 42 sts

Rounds 24–25: Using A, dc around. 42 sts

Round 26: As round 23. 42 sts
Attach safety eyes and embroider face.

Rounds 27–28: Using A, dc around. 42 sts

Round 29: As round 23. 42 sts

Rounds 30–31: Using A, dc around. 42 sts

Round 32: As round 23. 42 sts

Rounds 33–34: Using A, dc around. 42 sts

Round 35: As round 23. 42 sts

Round 36: Using A, dc around. 42 sts
Stuff head and body.

Round 37: Using A, dc around. 42 sts

Round 38: Using A, dc21, sl st to first dc to form a figure-of-eight for the tops of the legs. Work on the first half of this for the right leg.

Right leg

Rounds 39–42: Using A, dc around. 21 sts

Round 43: (dc in next dc, dc2tog) rep around. 11 sts

Round 44: (dc in next dc, dc2tog) rep around. 6 sts

Round 45: (dc in next dc, dc2tog) rep around. 3 sts
Break yarn and sew in tail.
Stuff right leg.

Left leg

Using A, pick up from st 22 of round 38 and work 21 dc around the second half of the figure-of-eight. Join to the first st using a sl st and work on these sts for the left leg.

Rounds 39–42: Dc around. 21 sts

Round 43: (dc in next dc, dc2tog) rep around. 11 sts

Round 44: (dc in next dc, dc2tog) rep around. 6 sts

Round 45: (dc in next dc, dc2tog) rep around. 3 sts
Break yarn and sew in tail.
Stuff left leg.

Round	Stitches	Yarn
1	MC 7	C
2	14 (inc 7)	C
3	21 (inc 7)	C
4	28 (inc 7)	C
5	35 (inc 7)	C
6	42 (inc 7)	C
7–20	42	C
Change to yellow and black (A and B)		
21–22	42	A
23	42	B, A B
24–25	42	A
26	42	B, A, B
27–28	42	A
29	42	B, A, B
30–31	42	A
32	42	B, A, B
33–34	42	A
35	42	B, A, B
36	42	A
Stuff head and body		
37	42	A
Begin right leg		
38 R	21	A
39–42 R	21	A
43 R	11 (dec 10)	A
44 R	6 (dec 4)	A
45 R	3 (dec 3)	A
Begin left leg		
38 L	21	A
39–42 L	21	A
43 L	11 (dec 10)	A
44 L	6 (dec 4)	A
45 L	3 (dec 3)	A

Rounds 13–14: Dc around. 8 sts
Change to B.
Round 15: Dc around. 8 sts
Change to A.
Rounds 16–17: Dc around. 8 sts
Change to B.
Round 18: Dc around. 8 sts
Change to A.
Rounds 19–20: Dc around. 8 sts
Fasten off and sew to body.

Round	Stitches	Yarn
1	MC 4	A
2	8 (inc 4)	A
3–8	8	A
9	8	B
10–11	8	A
12	8	B
13–14	8	A
15	8	B
16–17	8	A
18	8	B
19–20	8	A

Arms (make 2)

Round 1: Using A and MC, work 7 dc.
7 sts
Round 2: 2dc into each st. 14 sts
Rounds 3–8: Dc around. 14 sts
Break yarn, leaving a long tail.
Embroider fingers. Stuff arms lightly and
attach to body.

Round	Stitches	Yarn
1	MC 7	A
2	14 (inc 7)	A
3–8	14	A

Ears (make 2)

Round 1: Using A and MC, work 4 dc.
4 sts
Round 2: 2dc into each st. 8 sts
Round 3: Dc around. 8 sts
Round 4: (2dc in next dc, dc in next
3 dc) rep around. 10 sts
Round 5: (2dc in next dc, dc in next
4 dc) rep around. 12 sts
Fasten off, leaving a long tail.
Attach ears to head.

Round	Stitches	Yarn
1	MC 4	A
2	8 (inc 4)	A
3	8	A
4	10 (inc 2)	A
5	12 (inc 2)	A

Head stripes (make 3)

Using A, work 7ch and fasten off. Make
another the same.
Using A, make 15ch and fasten off.
Sew to head.

Tail

Round 1: Using A and MC, work 4 dc.
4 sts
Round 2: 2dc into each dc. 8 sts
Rounds 3–8: Dc around. 8 sts
Change to B
Round 9: Dc around. 8 sts
Change to A.
Rounds 10–11: Dc around. 8 sts
Change to B.
Round 12: Dc around. 8 sts
Change to A.

Plump and pretty, this soft plaything is sure to become a firm favourite – and the clear contrasts of black and white make this the ideal toy to capture the youngest child's attention.

Pandora Panda

Materials

Acrylic DK yarn

1 x 50g ball white (A)

Approx 25g black (B)

3mm crochet hook

Black embroidery yarn

Safety eyes

Stuffing

Black felt square and fabric adhesive (see note)

Special techniques

Magic circle (MC)

Double crochet (dc)

Increasing

Decreasing

Size

5in (12.5cm) high

Head (make 1)

Round 1: Using A and MC, work 6 dc. 6 sts

Round 2: 2dc into each dc. 12 sts

Round 3: (2dc in next dc, dc in next dc) rep around. 18 sts

Round 4: (2dc in next dc, dc in next 2 dc) rep around. 24 sts

Round 5: (2dc in next dc, dc in next 3 dc) rep around. 30 sts

Round 6: (2dc in next dc, dc in next 4 dc) rep around. 36 sts

Round 7: (2dc in next dc, dc in next 5 dc) rep around. 42 sts

Round 8: (2dc in next dc, dc in next 6 dc) rep around. 48 sts

Round 9: (2dc in next dc, dc in next 7 dc) rep around. 54 sts

Round 10: (2dc in next dc, dc in next 8 dc) rep around. 60 sts

Rounds 11–18: Dc around. 60 sts

Round 19: (dc in next 8 dc, dc2tog) rep around. 54 sts

Round 20: (dc in next 7 dc, dc2tog) rep around. 48 sts

Round 21: (dc in next 6 dc, dc2tog) rep around. 42 sts

Round 22: (dc in next 5 dc, dc2tog) rep around. 36 sts

Round 23: (dc in next 4 dc, dc2tog) rep around. 30 sts

Break yarn, leaving a long tail.

Round	Stitches	Yarn
1	MC 6	A
2	12 (inc 6)	A
3	18 (inc 6)	A
4	24 (inc 6)	A
5	30 (inc 6)	A
6	36 (inc 6)	A
7	42 (inc 6)	A
8	48 (inc 6)	A
9	54 (inc 6)	A
10	60 (inc 6)	A
11–18	60	A
19	54 (dec 6)	A
20	48 (dec 6)	A
21	42 (dec 6)	A
22	36 (dec 6)	A
23	30 (dec 6)	A

Body

Round 1: Using A and MC, work 6 dc. 6 sts

Round 2: 2dc into each st. 12 sts

Round 3: (2dc in next dc, dc in next dc) rep around. 18 sts

Round 4: (2dc in next dc, dc in next 2 dc) rep around. 24 sts

Round 5: (2dc in next dc, dc in next 3 dc) rep around. 30 sts

Round 6: (2dc in next dc, dc in next 4 dc) rep around. 36 sts

Round 7: (2dc in next dc, dc in next 5 dc) rep around. 42 sts

Rounds 8–9: Dc around. 42 sts

Round 10: (dc in next 5 dc, dc2tog) rep around. 36 sts

Round 11: Dc around. 36 sts

Round 12: (dc in next 4 dc, dc2tog) rep around. 30 sts

Rounds 13–14: Dc around. 30 sts

Break yarn, leaving a long tail.

Round	Stitches	Yarn
1	MC 6	A
2	12 (inc 6)	A
3	18 (inc 6)	A
4	24 (inc 6)	A
5	30 (inc 6)	A
6	36 (inc 6)	A
7	42 (inc 6)	A
8–9	42	A
10	36 (dec 6)	A
11	36	A
12	30 (dec 6)	A
13–14	30	A

Ears (make 2)

Round 1: Using B and MC, work 6 dc. 6 sts

Round 2: 2dc into each st, turn. 12 sts

Round 3: (2dc in next dc, dc in next dc) rep around, turn. 18 sts

Round 4: (2dc in next dc, dc in next 2 dc) rep around, turn. 24 sts

Rounds 5–7: Dc around, turn. 24 sts

Round 8: (dc in next 2 dc, dc2tog) rep around, turn. 18 sts

Round 9: Dc around. 18 sts

Break yarn, leaving a long tail.

Round	Stitches	Yarn
1	MC 6	B
2	12 (inc 6) turn	B
3	18 (inc 6) turn	B
4	24 (inc 6) turn	B
5–7	24 (turn)	B
8	18 (dec 6) turn	B
9	18	B

Arms (make 2)

Round 1: Using B and MC, work 6 dc. 6 sts

Round 2: 2dc into each st. 12 sts

Round 3: (dc in next 4 dc, 2 dc in next dc) rep around. 15 sts

Rounds 4–7: Dc around. 15 sts

Break yarn, leaving a long tail.

Round	Stitches	Yarn
1	MC 6	B
2	12 (inc 6)	B
3	15 (inc 3)	B
4–7	15	B

Legs (make 2)

Round 1: Using B and MC, work 6 dc. 6 sts

Round 2: 2dc into each st. 12 sts

Round 3: (dc in next 4 dc, 2dc in next dc) rep around. 15 sts

Rounds 4–5: Dc around. 15 sts

Round 6: Dc in next 12 dc, turn. 12 sts

Rounds 7–8: Rep row 6. 12 sts

Round 9: (dc in next 2 dc, dc2tog) rep twice, turn. 9 sts

Round 10: (dc in next dc, dc2tog) rep twice, turn. 6 sts

Round 11: (dc in next dc, dc2tog) rep once, turn. 4 sts

Round 12: Dc around all sts. 15 sts

Round 13: Dc around. 15 sts

Break yarn, leaving a long tail.

Round	Stitches	Yarn
1	MC 6	B
2	12 (inc 6)	B
3	15 (inc 3)	B
4–5	15	B
Shape foot		
6	12 (turn)	B
7–8	12 (turn)	B
9	9 (turn)	B
10	6 (turn)	B
11	4 (turn)	B
Work around all sts		
12	15	B
13	15	B

Tail

Round 1: Using B and MC, work 6 dc. 6 sts

Round 2: 2dc into each st. 12 sts

Round 3: Dc around. 12 sts

Round	Stitches	Yarn
1	MC 6	B
2	12 (inc 6)	B
3	12	B

Making up

Cut two large black felt ovals and two smaller white ovals for eyes. Make a hole in each piece for eyes to pass through and attach to head. Cut a felt oval for nose and glue or sew to head between eyes. Stuff all pieces. Attach ears, beg at row 5 from top of head. Sew limbs and head to body. Sew tail to back of body at row 5 from bottom. Sew in ends.

Note

If you do not wish to use felt for this toy, crochet small circles using black and white yarn and the magic circle technique, and use for the eye pieces.

Have you ever looked at a zebra in a zoo?
Then you'll know that they are not actually black and white, but more
off-white and grey – just like this gorgeous little playmate.

Zelda Zebra

Materials

Debbie Bliss Eco Cotton 100% organic cotton (90m per 50g)

1 x 50g ball grey (A)

1 x 50g ball off-white (B)

4mm crochet hook

Polyester stuffing

Black embroidery yarn

Safety eyes

Special techniques

Magic circle (MC)

Double crochet (dc)

Increasing

Decreasing

Size

7in (18cm) tall

Muzzle

Round 1: Using A and MC, work 5 dc. 5 sts

Round 2: 2dc into each dc. 10 sts

Round 3: (2dc in next dc, dc in next dc) rep around. 15 sts

Round 4: (2dc in next dc, dc in next 2dc) rep around. 20 sts

Rounds 5–6: Dc around. 20 sts
Break yarn, leaving a long tail.

Round	Stitches	Yarn
1	MC 5	A
2	10 (inc 5)	A
3	15 (inc 5)	A
4	20 (inc 5)	A
5–6	20	A

Head

Work in alt rounds of A and B.

Round 1: Using A and MC, work 5 dc. 5 sts

Round 2: 2dc into each st. 10 sts

Round 3: (2dc in next dc, dc in next dc) rep around. 15 sts

Round 4: (2dc in next dc, dc in next 2 dc) rep around. 20 sts

Round 5: (2dc in next dc, dc in next 3 dc) rep around. 25 sts

Rounds 6–12: Dc around. 25 sts

Round 13: (dc in next 3 dc, dc2tog) rep around. 20 sts

Attach eyes and stuff head. Stuff muzzle and join head and muzzle. Embroider mouth.

Round	Stitches	Yarn
1	MC 5	A
2	10 (inc 5)	B
3	15 (inc 5)	A
4	20 (inc 5)	B
5	25 (inc 5)	A
6–12	25	B
13	20 (dec 5)	A

Body

Work in alt rounds of A and B.

Round 1: Using A and MC, work 5 dc. 5 sts

Round 2: 2dc into each st. 10 sts

Round 3: (2dc in next dc, dc in next dc) rep around. 15 sts

Round 4: (2dc in next dc, dc in next 2 dc) rep around. 20 sts

Round 5: (2dc in next dc, dc in next 3 dc) rep around. 25 sts

Round 6: (2dc in next dc, dc in next 4 dc) rep around. 30 sts

Rounds 7–15: Dc around. 30 sts

Round 16: (dc in next 4 dc, dc2tog) rep around. 25 sts

Round 17: (dc in next 3 dc, dc2tog) rep around. 20 sts

Round 18: (dc in next 2 dc, dc2tog) rep around. 15 sts

Round 19: (dc in next dc, dc2tog) rep around. 10 sts

Round 20: (dc2tog) rep around. 5 sts
Work 2 sts into 1 until hole closes.

Round	Stitches	Yarn
1	MC 5	A
2	10 (inc 5)	B
3	15 (inc 5)	A
4	20 (inc 5)	B
5	25 (inc 5)	A
6	30 (inc 5)	B
7–15	30	alt A/B
16	25 (dec 5)	B
17	20 (dec 5)	A
18	15 (dec 5)	B
19	10 (dec 5)	A
20	5 (dec 5)	B

Legs (make 4)

Round 1: Using A and MC, work 4 dc. 4 sts

Round 2: 2dc into each st. 8 sts

Round 3: (2dc in next dc, dc in next dc) rep around. 12 sts

Rounds 4–6: Dc around. 12 sts
Now work in alt rounds of A and B, beg B.

Round 7: (dc in next 4dc, dc2tog) rep around. 10 sts

Rounds 8–14: Dc around. 10 sts

Round 15: 2dc into first st, dc rem sts. 11 sts
Break yarn, leaving a long tail.
Stuff legs and attach to body.

Round	Stitches	Yarn
1	15ch	B
2	15	A
3	15	B
4	15	A

Ears (make 2)

Round 1: Using B and MC, work 4 dc. 4 sts

Round 2: 2dc into each dc. 8 sts

Rounds 3–6: Dc around. 8 sts

Round 7: (dc2tog) rep around. 4 sts
Break yarn, leaving a long tail.
Attach ears to head.

Round	Stitches	Yarn
1	MC 4	B
2	8 (inc 4)	B
3–6	8	B
7	4 (dec 4)	B

Mane and tail

Knot yarn A down side of head and neck to form mane and cut to length. Braid lengths of A to form tail.

Round	Stitches	Yarn
1	MC 4	A
2	8 (inc 4)	A
3	12 (inc 4)	A
4–6	12	A
7	10 (dec 2)	B
8–14	10	alt A/B
15	11 (inc 1)	B

Neck

Work in alt rounds of A and B to form a tube, beg B:

Round 1: Make 15ch. 15 sts

Rounds 2–4: Dc around. 15 sts
Sew neck to head. Stuff neck and attach to body.

Note

This project is also featured in the Techniques section to illustrate the use of spiral charts (see pages 150–151).

This baby jumbo has packed her trunk and is all ready
to join in with some fun and games. She's sure to become
a plaything you'll never forget!

Ellie Elephant

Materials

Debbie Bliss Cashmerino Aran 55% merino wool
33% microfibre 12% cashmere (90m per 50g)
75g grey (A)
25g blue/grey (B)
3mm crochet hook
Black embroidery yarn
Toy eyes or black beads
Synthetic toy filling

Special techniques

Magic circle (MC)
Double crochet (dc)
Increasing
Decreasing

Size

9in (23cm) long, excluding tail

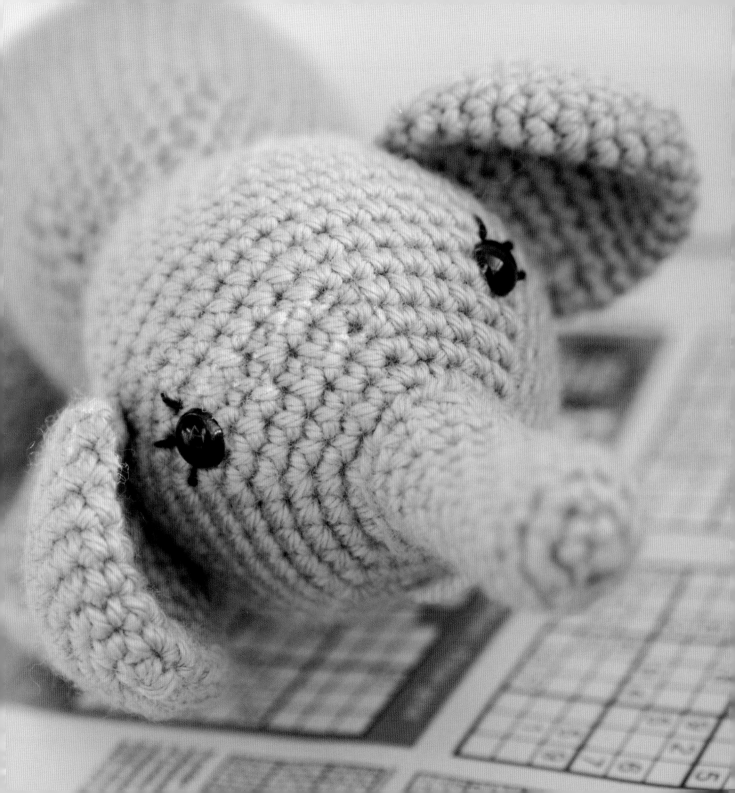

Head

Round 1: Using A and MC, work 5 dc. 5 sts

Round 2: Work 2 dc into each st. 10 sts

Round 3: (2dc in next dc, dc in next dc) rep around. 15 sts

Round 4: (2dc in next dc, dc in next 2 dc) rep around. 20 sts

Round 5: (2dc in next dc, dc in next 3 dc) rep around. 25 sts

Round 6: (2dc in next dc, dc in next 4 dc) rep around. 30 sts

Round 7: (2dc in next dc, dc in next 5 dc) rep around. 35 sts

Round 8: (2dc in next dc, dc in next 6 dc) rep around. 40 sts

Round 9: (2dc in next dc, dc in next 7 dc) rep around. 45 sts

Rounds 10–14: Dc around. 45 sts

Round 15: (dc in next 7 dc, dc2tog) rep around. 40 sts

Round 16: Dc around. 40 sts

Round 17: (dc in next 6 dc, dc2tog) rep around. 35 sts

Round 18: Dc around. 35 sts

Round 19: (dc in next 5 dc, dc2tog) rep around. 30 sts

Round 20: (dc in next 4 dc, dc2tog) rep around. 25 sts

Break yarn, leaving a long tail.

Round	Stitches	Yarn
1	MC 5	A
2	10 (inc 5)	A
3	15 (inc 5)	A
4	20 (inc 5)	A
5	25 (inc 5)	A
6	30 (inc 5)	A
7	35 (inc 5)	A
8	40 (inc 5)	A
9	45 (inc 5)	A
10–14	45	A
15	40 (dec 5)	A
16	40	A
17	35 (dec 5)	A
18	35	A
19	30 (dec 5)	A
20	25 (dec 5)	A

Ears (make 2)

Round 1: Using A and MC, work 5 dc. 5 sts

Round 2: 2dc into each st. 10 sts

Round 3: (2dc in next dc, dc in next dc) rep around. 15 sts

Round 4: (2dc in next dc, dc in next 2 dc) rep around. 20 sts

Round 5: (2dc in next dc, dc in next 3 dc) rep around. 25 sts

Rounds 6–9: Dc around. 25 sts

Round 10: (dc in next 3 dc, dc2tog) rep around. 20 sts

Round 11: (dc in next 2 dc, dc2tog) rep around. 15 sts

Round	Stitches	Yarn
1	MC 5	A
2	10 (inc 5)	A
3	15 (inc 5)	A
4	20 (inc 5)	A
5	25 (inc 5)	A
6–9	25	A
10	20 (dec 5)	A
11	15 (dec 5)	A

Body (make 1)

Round 1: Using A and MC, work 5 dc. 5 sts

Round 2: 2dc into each dc. 10 sts

Round 3: (2dc in next dc, dc in next dc) rep around. 15 sts

Round 4: (2dc in next dc, dc in next 2 dc) rep around. 20 sts

Round 5: (2dc in next dc, dc in next 3 dc) rep around. 25 sts

Round 6: (2dc in next dc, dc in next 4 dc) rep around. 30 sts

Round 7: (2dc in next dc, dc in next 5 dc) rep around. 35 sts

Round 8: (2dc in next dc, dc in next 6 dc) rep around. 40 sts

Round 9: (2dc in next dc, dc in next 7 dc) rep around. 45 sts

Rounds 10–15: Dc around. 45 sts

Round 16: (dc in next 7 dc, dc2tog) rep around. 40 sts

Rounds 17–18: Dc around. 40 sts

Round 19: (2dc in next dc, dc in next 7 dc) rep around. 45 sts

Rounds 20–24: Dc around. 45 sts

Round 25: (dc in next 7 dc, dc2tog) rep around. 40 sts

Round 26: (dc in next 6 dc, dc2tog) rep around. 35 sts

Round 27: (dc in next 5 dc, dc2tog) rep around. 30 sts

Round 28: (dc in next 4 dc, dc2tog) rep around. 25 sts

Break yarn, leaving a long tail.

Round	Stitches	Yarn
1	MC 5	A
2	10 (inc 5)	A
3	15 (inc 5)	A
4	20 (inc 5)	A
5	25 (inc 5)	A
6	30 (inc 5)	A
7	35 (inc 5)	A
8	40 (inc 5)	A
9	45 (inc 5)	A
10–15	45	A
16	40 (dec 5)	A
17–18	40	A
19	45 (inc 5)	A
20–24	45	A
25	40 (dec 5)	A
26	35 (dec 5)	A
27	30 (dec 5)	A
28	25 (dec 5)	A

Legs (make 4)

Round 1: Using B and MC, work 5 dc. 5 sts

Round 2: 2dc into each dc. 10 sts

Round 3: (2dc in next dc, dc in next dc) rep around. 15 sts

Change to A.

Rounds 4–12: Dc around. 15 sts
Break yarn, leaving a long tail.

Round	Stitches	Yarn
1	MC 5	B
2	10 (inc 5)	B
3	15 (inc 5)	B
4–12	15	A

Trunk (make 1)

Round 1: Using A and MC, work 5 dc. 5 sts

Round 2: 2dc into each st. 10 sts

Rounds 3–11: Dc around. 10 sts

Round 12: (2dc in next dc, dc in next 4 dc) rep around. 12 sts

Break yarn, leaving a long tail.

Round	Stitches	Yarn
1	MC 5	A
2	10 (inc 5)	A
3–11	10	A
12	12 (inc 2)	A

Tail

Cut 3 x 4in (10cm) strands of A and braid together. Tie loose ends together to form bush of tail.

Making up

Attach trunk to head, using centre of round 1 as guide. Sew on ears, making sure they line up. Attach eyes, 4 rounds from centre of trunk. Embroider mouth. Stuff limbs and attach to body. Attach tail. Stuff body. Sew head to body.

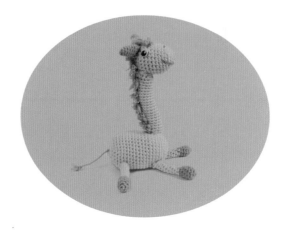

She may be a little unsteady on her spindly legs, but this little lady is willing to stick her neck out and insist that she's the most gorgeous giraffe ever to grace a nursery.

Gemma Giraffe

Materials

Debbie Bliss Cashmerino Aran 55% merino wool
33% microfibre 12% cashmere (90m per 50g)
2 x 50g balls yellow (A)
1 x 50g ball orange (B)
3mm and 3.5mm crochet hooks
Black embroidery yarn
Toy eyes or black beads
Polyester stuffing

Special techniques

Magic circle (MC)
Double crochet
Increasing
Decreasing

Size

10in (25cm) tall

Head

Round 1: Using 3.5mm hook, A and MC, work 5 dc. 5 sts

Round 2: 2dc into each st. 10 sts

Round 3: (2dc in next dc, dc in next dc) rep around. 15 sts

Round 4: (2dc in next dc, dc in next 2dc) rep around. 20 sts

Round 5: Dc around. 20 sts

Round 6: (2dc in next dc, dc in next 3 dc) rep around. 25 sts

Rounds 7–12: Dc around. 25 sts

Round 13: (dc in next 3dc, dc2tog) rep around. 20 sts

Round 14: (dc in next 2dc, dc2tog) rep around. 15 sts

Attach eyes, embroider mouth and nose, stuff.

Round 15: (dc in next dc, dc2tog) rep around. 10 sts

Round 16: (dc2tog) rep around. 5 sts

Work 2 sts into 1 until hole closes. Fasten off and sew in tail.

Round	Stitches	Yarn
1	MC 5	A
2	10 (inc 5)	A
3	15 (inc 5)	A
4	20 (inc 5)	A
5	20	A
6	25 (inc 5)	A
7–12	25	A
13	20	A
14	15	A
Attach eyes, embroider mouth and nose and stuff		
15	10 (dec 5)	A
16	5 (dec 5)	A

Neck

Round 1: Using 3.5mm hook and A, work 13ch. Sl st to st 1 to form a loop. 13 sts

Rounds 2–21: Dc around. 13 sts
Break yarn, leaving a long tail.

Round	Stitches	Yarn
1	13ch	A
2–21	13	A

Body

Round 1: Using 3.5mm hook, A and MC, work 5dc. 5 sts

Round 2: 2dc into each st. 10 sts

Round 3: (2dc in next dc, dc in next dc) rep around. 15 sts

Round 4: (2dc in next dc, dc in next 2 dc) rep around. 20 sts

Round 5: (2dc in next dc, dc in next 3 dc) rep around. 25 sts

Round 6: (2dc in next dc, dc in next 4 dc) rep around. 30 sts

Round 7: (2dc in next dc, dc in next 5 dc) rep around. 35 sts

Rounds 8–19: Dc around. 35 sts

Round 20: (dc in next 5 dc, dc2tog) rep around. 30 sts

Round 21: (dc in next 4 dc, dc2tog) rep around. 25 sts

Round 22: (dc in next 3 dc, dc2tog) rep around. 20 sts

Round 23: (dc in next 2 dc, dc2tog) rep around. 15 sts

Stuff toy.

Round 24: (dc in next dc, dc2tog) rep around. 10 sts

Round 25: (dc2tog) rep around. 5 sts

Work 2 sts into 1 until hole closes. Fasten off and darn in yarn end.

Round	Stitches	Yarn
1	MC 5	A
2	10 (inc 5)	A
3	15 (inc 5)	A
4	20 (inc 5)	A
5	25 (inc 5)	A
6	30 (inc 5)	A
7	35 (inc 5)	A
8–19	35	A
20	30 (dec 5)	A
21	25 (dec 5)	A
22	20 (dec 5)	A
23	15 (dec 5)	A
Stuff		
24	10 (dec 5)	A
25	5 (dec 5)	A

Legs (make 4)

Round 1: Using B and MC, work 4 dc. 4 sts

Round 2: (2dc into each dc) rep around. 8 sts

Rounds 3–5: Dc around. 8 sts

Round 6: (dc in next 2 dc, dc2tog) rep around. 6 sts

Change to A.

Rounds 7–16: Dc around. 6 sts

Break yarn, leaving a long tail.

Round	Stitches	Yarn
1	MC 4	B
2	8 (inc 4)	B
3–5	8	B
6	6 (dec 2)	B
7–16	6	A

Ears (make 2)

Round 1: Using 3mm hook, B and MC, work 4 dc. 4 sts

Round 2: 2dc into each st. 8 sts

Rounds 3–7: Dc around. 8 sts

Round 8: (dc2tog) rep around. 4 sts

Break yarn, leaving a long tail.

Round	Stitches	Yarn
1	MC 4	B
2	8 (inc 4)	B
3–7	8	B
8	4 (dec 4)	B

Horns (make 2)

Using several strands of B, tie a knot to represent a giraffe's small bumpy horns. Sew to head above eyes.

Making up

Sew ears to head above eyes. Sew neck to head, stuff neck very firmly and attach to body. Attach legs to body.

Mane and tail

Thread three lengths of B through body and braid to form tail. Thread lengths of yarn though top of head and knot to form mane.

Amigurumi is so addictive that you could end up with quite a collection. Where better to stash your work-in-progress than this gorgeous bag? It also makes a fun shopper.

Bear Bag

Materials

Sirdar Click Chunky 30% wool 70% acrylic (75m per 50g)

2 x 50g balls shade 131 Heather (A)

1 x 50g ball shade 147 Loom Blue (B)

Debbie Bliss Cashmerino Aran 55% merino wool
33% microfibre 12% cashmere (90m per 25g)

10g beige (C)

5g light brown (D)

3.5 and 4.5mm crochet hooks

Black embroidery thread

Special techniques

Magic circle (MC)

Double crochet (dc)

Increasing

Decreasing

Size

8in (20cm) wide x 8in (20cm) deep, excluding handle

Bag

Round 1: Using 4.5mm hook, B and MC, work 5 dc. 5 sts

Round 2: 2dc into each st. 10 sts

Round 3: (2dc in next dc, dc in next dc) rep around. 15 sts

Round 4: (2dc in next dc, dc in next 2 dc) rep around. 20 sts

Round 5: (2dc in next dc, dc in next 3 dc) rep around. 25 sts

Round 6: (2dc in next dc, dc in next 4 dc) rep around. 30 sts

Round 7: (2dc in next dc, dc in next 5 dc) rep around. 35 sts

Round 8: (2dc in next dc, dc in next 6 dc) rep around. 40 sts

Round 9: (2dc in next dc, dc in next 7 dc) rep around. 45 sts

Round 10: Dc around. 45 sts
Change to A.

Round 11: (2dc in next dc, dc in next 8 dc) rep around. 50 sts

Round 12: Dc around. 50 sts

Round 13: (2dc in next dc, dc in next 9 dc) rep around. 55 sts

Rounds 14–15: Dc around. 55 sts

Round 16: (2dc in next dc, dc in next 10 dc) rep around. 60 sts

Round 17: Dc around. 60 sts

Round 18: 2dc in next dc, dc in next 30 dc, 2dc in next dc, dc rem sts. 62 sts

Round 19: Dc around. 62 sts

Round 20: 2dc in next dc, dc 31, 2dc in next dc, dc rem sts. 64 sts

Round 21: Dc around. 64 sts

Round 22: 2dc in next 2 dc, dc in next 32 dc, 2dc in next 2 dc, dc rem sts. 68 sts

Round 23: Dc around. 68 sts

Round	Stitches	Yarn
1	MC 5	B
2	10 (inc 5)	B
3	15 (inc 5)	B
4	20 (inc 5)	B
5	25 (inc 5)	B
6	30 (inc 5)	B
7	35 (inc 5)	B
8	40 (inc 5)	B
9	45 (inc 5)	B
10	45	B
Change to A		
11	50 (inc 5)	A
12	50	A
13	55 (inc 5)	A
14–15	55	A
16	60 (inc 5)	A
17	60	A
18	62 (inc 2)	A
19	62	A
20	64 (inc 2)	A
21	64	A
22	68 (inc 4)	A
23	68	A
24	70 (inc 2)	A
25	70	A
26	72 (inc 2)	A
27	72	A
28	74 (inc 2)	A
29	74	A
30	76 (inc 2)	A
31–40	76	A
Change to B		
41–44	76	B

Round 24: 2dc in next dc, dc in next 33 dc, 2dc in next dc, dc rem sts. 70 sts

Round 25: Dc around. 70 sts

Round 26: 2dc in next dc, dc in next 34 dc, 2dc in next dc, dc rem sts. 72 sts

Round 27: Dc around. 72 sts

Round 28: 2dc in next dc, dc in next 35 dc, 2dc in next dc, dc rem sts. 74 sts

Round 29: Dc around. 74 sts

Round 30: 2dc in next dc, dc in next 36 dc, 2dc in next dc, dc rem sts. 76 sts

Rounds 31–40: Dc around. 76 sts
Change to B.

Rounds 41–44: Dc around. 76 sts
Break yarn, leaving a long tail.

Bear face

Round 1: Using 3.5mm hook, C and MC, work 8 dc. 8 sts

Round 2: 2dc into each st. 16 sts

Round 3: (2dc in next dc, dc in next dc) rep around. 24 sts

Round 4: (dc 3, 3dc into next dc, dc 7, 3dc into next dc) rep around. 32 sts

Round 5: (dc 5, 3dc into next dc, dc 9, 3dc into next dc) rep around. 40 sts

Round 6: Dc 2, 3dc into next dc, dc 21, 3dc into next dc, dc 16. 44 sts

Round 7: Dc around. 44 sts
Break yarn, leaving a long tail.

Muzzle

Round 1: Using 3.5mm hook, D and MC, work 8 dc. 8 sts

Round 2: 2dc into each st. 16 sts

Round 3: (dc 2, 3dc in next dc, dc 4, 3dc into next dc) rep around. 24 sts

Round 4: Dc 1, 2dc into next st, dc 10, 2dc into next dc, dc 11. 26 sts
Break yarn, leaving a long tail.

Round	Stitches	Yarn
1	MC 8	D
2	16 (inc 8)	D
3	24 (inc 8)	D
4	26 (inc 2)	D

Ears (make 2)

Round 1: Using 3.5mm hook, C and MC, work 4 dc. 4 sts

Round 2: 2dc into each st. 8 sts

Round 3: (2dc in next dc, dc in next dc) rep around. 12 sts

Rounds 4–5: Dc around. 12 sts
Fasten off, leaving a long tail.

Round	Stitches	Yarn
1	MC 4	C
2	8 (inc 4)	C
3	12 (inc 4)	C
4–5	12	C

Making up

Embroider nose and mouth on muzzle. Stuff muzzle lightly and sew to head. Embroider eyes. Sew bear face to bag, stuffing lightly. Attach ears.

Round	Stitches	Yarn
1	MC 8	C
2	16 (inc 8)	C
3	24 (inc 8)	C
4	32 (inc 8)	C
5	40 (inc 8)	C
6	44 (inc 4)	C
7	44	C

Handles

Using 4.5mm hook and B, make 8ch and sl st to form a ring.
Work in rounds of dc to form a tube until handle measures 12in (30cm) or length required. Attach to inside of bag.

Rats may not be anyone's first choice for a playtime companion, but this cuddly character is so dashing that he should easily dispel any fear of rodents.

Rakish Rat

Materials

Debbie Bliss Cashmerino Aran 55% merino wool
33% microfibre 12% cashmere (90m per 25g)
2 x 25g balls dark grey (A)
1 x 25g ball pink or beige (B)
1 x 25g ball red (C)
3mm and 3.5mm crochet hooks
Black embroidery yarn
Toy eyes
Polyester stuffing
3 small buttons

Special techniques

Magic circle (MC)
Double crochet (dc)
Increasing
Decreasing

Size

10in (25cm) tall

Muzzle

Round 1: Using 3.5mm hook, A and MC, work 5dc. 5 sts

Round 2: 2dc into each dc. 10 sts

Round 3: (2dc in next dc, dc in next dc) rep around. 15 sts

Round 4: (2dc in next dc, dc in next 3 dc) rep around. 20 sts

Round 5: (2dc in next dc, dc in next 4 dc) dc around. 25 sts

Round 6: Dc around. 25 sts

Round 7: (2dc in next dc, dc in next 5 dc) rep around. 30 sts

Rounds 8–9: Dc around. 30 sts

Break yarn, leaving a long tail.

Round	Stitches	Yarn
1	MC 5	A
2	10 (inc 5)	A
3	15 (inc 5)	A
4	20 (inc 5)	A
5	25 (inc 5)	A
6	25	A
7	30 (inc 5)	A
8–9	30	A

Head

Round 1: Using 3.5mm hook, A and MC, work 6 dc. 6 sts

Round 2: 2dc into each st. 12 sts

Round 3: (2dc in next dc, dc in next dc) rep around. 18 sts

Round 4: (2dc in next dc, dc in next 2 dc) rep around. 24 sts

Round 5: (2dc in next dc, dc in next 3 dc) rep around. 30 sts

Round 6: (2dc in next dc, dc in next 4 dc) rep around. 36 sts

Round 7: (2dc in next dc, dc next 5 dc) rep around. 42 sts

Round 8: (2dc in next dc, dc next 6 dc) rep around. 48 sts

Rounds 9–18: Dc around. 48 sts

Round 19: (dc next 6 dc, dc2tog) rep around. 42 sts

Round 20: (dc next 5 dc, dc2tog) rep around. 36 sts

Round 21: (dc next 4 dc, dc2tog) rep around. 30 sts

Round 22: (dc next 3 dc, dc2tog) rep around. 24 sts

Break yarn, leaving a long tail.

Round	Stitches	Yarn
1	MC 6	A
2	12 (inc 6)	A
3	18 (inc 6)	A
4	24 (inc 6)	A
5	30 (inc 6)	A
6	36 (inc 6)	A
7	42 (inc 6)	A
8	48 (inc 6)	A
9–18	48	A
19	42 (dec 6)	A
20	36 (dec 6)	A
21	30 (dec 6)	A
22	24 (dec 6)	A

Nose

Round 1: Using 3.5mm hook, B and MC, work 4 dc. 4sts

Round 2: 2dc into each dc. 8 sts

Break yarn, leaving a long tail.

Sew to muzzle, stuff muzzle lightly and attach to head. Embroider mouth.

Body

Round 1: Using 3.5mm hook, A and MC work 6 dc. 6 sts

Round 2: (2dc into each dc) rep around. 12 sts

Round 3: (2dc in next dc, dc in next dc) rep around. 18 sts

Round 4: (2dc in next dc, dc in next 2 dc) rep around. 24 sts

Round 5: (2dc in next dc, dc in next 3 dc) rep around. 30 sts

Round 6: (2dc in next dc, dc in next 4 dc) rep around. 36 sts

Round 7: (2dc in next dc, dc in next 5 dc) rep around. 42 sts

Rounds 8–10: Dc around. 42 sts
Change to C.

Round 11: Dc around. 42 sts

Round 12: Dc around, working into front of sts of row 11. 42 sts

Round 13: Dc around, working into back of sts of row 11. 42 sts

Rounds 14–16: Dc around. 42 sts

Round 17: (dc2tog, dc in next 19 dc) rep twice. 40 sts

Round 18: (dc2tog, dc in next 18 dc) rep twice. 38 sts

Round 19: (dc2tog, dc in next 17 dc) rep twice. 36 sts

Round 20: (dc2tog, dc in next 10 dc) rep three times. 33 sts

Round 21: (dc2tog, dc in next 9 dc) rep three times. 30 sts

Round 22: (dc2tog, dc in next 8 dc) rep three times. 27 sts

Round 23: (dc2tog, dc7 into front of sts) rep three times. 24 sts

Rounds 24–26: Dc around. 24 sts
Break yarn, leaving a long tail.

Round	Stitches	Yarn
1	MC 6	A
2	12 (inc 6)	A
3	18 (inc 6)	A
4	24 (inc 6)	A
5	30 (inc 6)	A
6	36 (inc 6)	A
7	42 (inc 6)	A
8–10	42	A
11	42	C
12	42 in front of sts	C
13	42 in front of sts	C
14–16	42	C
17	40 (dec 2)	C
18	38 (dec 2)	C
19	36 (dec 2)	C
20	33 (dec 3)	C
21	30 (dec 3)	C
22	27 (dec 3)	C
23	24 in front (dec 3)	C
24–26	24	C

Legs (make 2)

Round 1: Using 3.5mm hook, B and MC, work 5 dc. 5 sts

Round 2: 2dc into each dc. 10 sts

Round 3: (2dc in next dc, dc1) rep around. 15 sts

Rounds 4–5: Dc around. 15 sts

Round 6: (dc2tog in next dc, dc into next dc) rep around. 10 sts
Change to A.

Rounds 7–20: Dc around. 10 sts
Break yarn, leaving a long tail.

Round	Stitches	Yarn
1	MC 5	B
2	10 (inc 5)	B
3	15 (inc 5)	B
4–5	15	B
6	10 (dec 5)	B
7–20	10	A

Ears (1 grey, 1 beige)

Round 1: Using 3.5mm hook and MC, work 8 dc. 8 sts

Round 2: 2dc into each st. 16 sts

Round 3: (2dc in next dc, dc into next dc) rep around. 24 sts

Round 4: (2dc in next dc, dc into next 2 dc) rep around. 32 sts

Rounds 5–10: Dc around. 32 sts

Round 11: (dc2tog, dc into next 2 dc) eight times. 24 sts

Round 12: (dc2tog, dc into next dc) rep around. 18 sts

Rounds 13–14: Dc around. 18 sts
Break yarn, leaving a long tail.

Round	Stitches	Yarn
1	MC 8	A or B
2	16 (inc 8)	A or B
3	24 (inc 8)	A or B
4	32 (inc 8)	A or B
5–10	32	A or B
11	24 (dec 8)	A or B
12	18 (dec 6)	A or B
13–14	18	A or B

Arms (make 2)

Round 1: Using 3.5mm hook, A and MC, work 5 dc. 5 sts

Round 2: 2dc into each dc. 10 sts

Round 3: (2dc in next dc, dc into next dc) rep around. 15 sts

Rounds 4–5: Dc around. 15 sts

Round 6: (dc2tog in next dc, dc into next dc) rep around. 10 sts
Change to C.

Round 7: Dc into front of sts. 10 sts

Round 8: Dc into back of sts. 10 sts

Rounds 9–20: Dc around. 10 sts
Break yarn, leaving a long tail.

Round	Stitches	Yarn
1	MC 5	A
2	10 (inc 5)	A
3	15 (inc 5)	A
4–5	15	A
6	10 (dec 5)	A
7	10 in front of sts	C
8	10 in back of sts	C
9–20	10	C

Tail

Round 1: Using 3mm hook, A and MC, work 3 dc. 3 sts

Round 2: 2dc into each st. 6 sts
Work 14 rounds dc on these 6 sts.
Break yarn, leaving a long tail.

Making up

Stuff limbs and tail and sew to body. Attach ears, eyes and buttons. Stuff head and sew to body.

Who's the coolest cat around in his best red trousers and matching braces? It's no wonder that this funky feline is smiling: he feels as though he just got all the cream.

Cute Cat

Materials

Debbie Bliss Cashmerino Aran 55% merino wool
33% microfibre 12% cashmere (90m per 50g)
1 x 50g ball light brown (A)
1 x 50g ball white (B)
Approx 25g red (C)
3.5mm crochet hook
Polyester stuffing
Black embroidery thread
2 small black buttons
Safety eyes

Special techniques

Magic circle (MC)
Double crochet (dc)
Increasing
Decreasing

Size

10in (25cm) tall

Head

Round 1: Using A and MC, work 6 dc. 6 sts

Round 2: 2dc into each st. 12 sts

Round 3: (2dc in next dc, dc in next dc) rep around. 18 sts

Round 4: (2dc in next dc, dc in next 2 dc) rep around. 24 sts

Round 5: (2dc in next dc, dc in next 3 dc) rep around. 30 sts

Round 6: (2dc in next dc, dc in next 4 dc) rep around. 36 sts

Round 7: (2dc in next dc, dc in next 5 dc) rep around. 42 sts

Cont in rounds of dc on these 42 sts, foll diagram if preferred:

Round 8: Dc 14A, 2B, 9A, 2B, 15A.

Round 9: Dc 13A, 4B, 7A, 4B, 14A.

Round 10: Dc 12A, 6B, 5A, 6B, 13A.

Round 11: Dc 11A, 8B, 3A, 8B, 12A.

Round 12: Dc 10A, 10B, 1A, 10B, 11A.

Round 13: Dc 10A, 21B, 11A.

Round 14: Dc 10A, 21B, 11A.

Round 15: Dc 10A, 21B, 11A.

Round 16: Dc 10A, 21B, 11A.

Round 17: (dc2tog, dc in next 5 dc) working 8A, 19B, 9A. 36 sts

Round 18: (dc2tog, dc in next 4 dc) working 6A, 17B, 7A. 30 sts

Round 19: (dc2tog, dc in next 3 dc) working 4A, 15B, 5A. 24 sts

Round 20: (dc2tog, dc in next 2 dc) working 4A, 9B, 5A. 18 sts

Fasten off, leaving a long tail. Embroider face, attach eyes. Stuff.

Round	Stitches	Yarn
1	MC 6	A
2	12 (inc 6)	A
3	18 (inc 6)	A
4	24 (inc 6)	A
5	30 (inc 6)	A
6	36 (inc 6)	A
7	42 (inc 6)	A
8–16	42	see chart
17	36 (dec 6)	see chart
18	30 (dec 6)	see chart
19	24 (dec 6)	see chart
20	18 (dec 6)	see chart

Body

Round 1: Using C and MC, work 5 dc. 5 sts

Round 2: 2dc into each st. 10 sts

Round 3: (2dc in next dc, dc in next dc) rep around. 15 sts

Round 4: (2dc in next dc, dc in next 2 dc) rep around. 20 sts

Round 5: (2dc in next dc, dc in next 3 dc) rep around. 25 sts

Round 6: (2dc in next dc, dc in next 4 dc) rep around. 30 sts

Round 7: (2dc in next dc, dc in next 5 dc) rep around. 35 sts

Rounds 8–12: Dc around. 35 sts Change to A.

Rounds 13–16: Dc around. 35 sts

Round 17: (dc in next 5 dc, dc2tog) rep around. 30 sts

Round 18: Dc around. 30 sts

Round 19: (dc in next 4 dc, dc2tog) rep around. 25 sts

Round 20: Dc around. 25 sts

Round 21: (dc in next 3 dc, dc2tog) rep around. 20 sts

Round 22: Dc around. 20 sts

Round 23: (dc in next 8 dc, dc2tog) rep around. 18 sts

Round 24: Dc around. 18 sts

Fasten off, leaving a long tail.

Round	Stitches	Yarn
1	MC 5	C
2	10 (inc 5)	C
3	15 (inc 5)	C
4	20 (inc 5)	C
5	25 (inc 5)	C
6	30 (inc 5)	C
7	35 (inc 5)	C
8–12	35	C
Change to A		
13–16	35	A
17	30 (dec 5)	A
18	30	A
19	25 (dec 5)	A
20	25	A
21	20 (dec 5)	A
22	20	A
23	18 (dec 2)	A
24	18	A

Ears (make 2)

Round 1: Using A and MC, work 4 dc. 4 sts

Round 2: 2dc into each st. 8 sts

Round 3: (2dc in next dc, dc in next dc) rep around. 12 sts

Rounds 4–5: Dc around. 12 sts

Break yarn, leaving a long tail.

Arms (make 2)

Round 1: Using B and MC, work 4 dc. 4 sts

Round 2: 2dc into each st. 8 sts

Round 3: (2dc in next dc, dc in next 3 dc) rep around. 10 sts

Rounds 4–6: Dc around. 10 sts

Round 7: (dc in next 3 dc, dc2tog) rep around. 8 sts

Change to A.

Rounds 8–17: Dc around. 8 sts

Break yarn, leaving a long tail.

Round	Stitches	Yarn
1	MC 4	B
2	8 (inc 4)	B
3	10 (inc 2)	B
4–6	10	B
7	8 (dec 2)	B
8–17	8	A

Legs (make 2)

Round 1: Using B and MC work 4 dc. 4 sts

Round 2: 2dc into each st. 8 sts

Round 3: (2dc in next dc, dc in next dc) rep around. 12 sts

Round 4: (2dc in next 2 dc, dc in next dc) rep around. 16 sts

Rounds 5–7: Dc around. 16 sts

Round 8: (dc in next 2 dc, dc2tog) rep around. 12 sts

Change to A.

Rounds 9–12: Dc around. 12 sts

Round 13: Dc2tog in the next st; dc around rem sts. 11 sts

Rounds 14–16: Dc around. 11 sts

Change to C.

Round 17: Dc2tog in the next st; dc around rem sts. 10 sts

Rounds 18–20: Dc around. 10 sts

Round 21: Dc2tog in the next st; dc around rem sts. 9 sts

Rounds 22–24: Dc around. 9 sts

Break yarn, leaving a long tail.

Round	Stitches	Yarn
1	MC 4	B
2	8 (inc 4)	B
3	12 (inc 4)	B
4	16 (inc 4)	B
5–7	16	B
8	12 (dec 4)	B
9–12	12	A
13	11 (dec 1)	A
14–16	11	A
17	10 (dec 1)	C
18–20	10	C
21	9 (dec 1)	C
22–24	9	C

Tail

Round 1: Using A and MC, work 5 dc. 5 sts

Rounds 2–20: Dc around. 5 sts

Fasten off, leaving a long tail.

Round	Stitches	Yarn
1	MC 5	A
2-20	5	A

Braces (make 2)

Round 1: Using C, make 25ch.

Round 2: Dc into each ch.

Fasten off, leaving a long tail.

Making up

Stuff body and sew to head. Stuff limbs and tail and sew to body. Attach ears. Sew braces to body, hooking over shoulders. Attach buttons to braces.

Cat head chart   42 sts and 20 rows

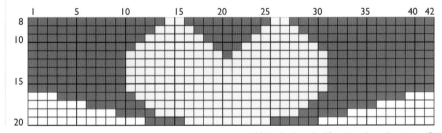

Note: chart worked from top down, beg at row 8.

Swimming serenely and smiling his secret smile,
Sebastian the sea-green stunner seems to be saying that
he's the smartest seahorse in all the seven seas.

Sebastian Seahorse

Materials

Debbie Bliss Cashmerino Aran 55% merino wool
33% microfibre 12% cashmere (90m per 25g)
1 x 50g ball dark green (A)
1 x 50g ball light green (B)
25g medium green (C)
3mm crochet hook
Polyester stuffing
Black embroidery thread
Large safety eyes

Special techniques

Magic circle (MC)
Double crochet (dc)
Increasing
Decreasing

Size

10in (25cm) tall

Body

Round 1: Using A and MC, work 8 dc. 8 sts

Rounds 2–10: Dc around. 8 sts
Change to B.

Round 11: 2dc into next dc, dc rem sts. 9 sts

Round 12: Dc around. 9 sts
Change to A.

Rounds 13–15: Dc around. 9 sts.
Change to B.

Round 16: 2dc into next dc, dc rem sts. 10 sts

Round 17: Dc around. 10 sts
Change to A.

Rounds 18–20: Dc around. 10 sts
Change to B.

Rounds 21–22: Dc around. 10 sts
Change to A.

Rounds 23–25: Dc around. 10 sts
Change to B.

Round 26: 2dc into next dc, dc rem sts. 11 sts

Round 27: Dc around. 11 sts
Change to A.

Rounds 28–30: Dc around. 10 sts
Change to B.

Round 31: 2dc into next dc, dc rem sts. 12 sts

Round 32: Dc around. 12 sts
Change to A.

Rounds 33–35: Dc around. 12 sts
Change to B.

Round 36: 2dc into each of next 2 dc; 8dc; 2dc into each of next 2 dc. 16 sts

Round 37: Dc around. 16 sts
Change to A.

Round 38: 2dc into each of next 2 dc; dc next 12 dc; 2dc into each of next 2 dc. 20 sts

Rounds 39–40: Dc around. 20 sts
Change to B.

Round 41: 2dc into each of next 2 dc, dc next 16 dc, 2dc into each of next 2 dc. 24 sts

Round 42: Dc around. 24 sts
Change to A.

Round 43: 2dc into each of next 2 dc, dc next 20 dc, 2dc into each of next 2 dc. 28 sts

Rounds 44–45: Dc around. 28 sts

Change to B.

Round 46: 2dc into each of next 2 dc, dc next 24 dc, 2dc into each of next 2 dc. 32 sts

Round 47: Dc around. 32 sts
Change to A.

Rounds 48–50: Dc around. 32 sts
Change to B

Rounds 51–52: Dc around. 32 sts
Change to A.

Rounds 53–55: Dc around. 32 sts
Change to B.

Round 56: (dc2tog) twice, dc next 24 dc, (dc2tog) twice. 28 sts

Round 57: Dc around. 28 sts
Change to A.

Round	Stitches	Yarn	Round	Stitches	Yarn
1	MC 8	A	41	24 (inc 4)	B
2–10	8	A	42	24	B
11	9 (inc 1)	B	43	28 (inc 4)	A
12	9	B	44–45	28	A
13–15	9	A	46	32 (inc 4)	B
16	10 (inc 1)	B	47	32	B
17	10	B	48–50	32	A
18–20	10	A	51–52	32	B
21–22	10	B	53–55	32	A
23–25	10	A	56	28 (dec 4)	B
26	11 (inc 1)	B	57	28	B
27	11	B	58	24 (dec 4)	A
28–30	11	A	59–60	24	A
31	12 (inc 1)	B	61	20 (dec 4)	B
32	12	B	62	20	B
33–35	12	A	63	16 (dec 4)	A
36	16 (inc 4)	B	64	14 (dec 2)	A
37	16	B	65	12 (dec 2)	A
38	20 (inc 4)	A	66–67	12	A
39–40	20	A			

Round 58: (dc2tog) twice, dc next 20 dc, (dc2tog) twice. 24 sts

Rounds 59–60: Dc around. 24 sts Stuff.

Round 61: (dc2tog) twice, dc next 16 dc, (dc2tog) twice. 20 sts

Round 62: Dc around. 20 sts

Round 63: (dc2tog) twice, dc next 12 dc, (dc2tog) twice. 16 sts

Round 64: Dc2tog, dc next 12 dc, dc2tog. 14 sts

Round 65: Dc2tog, dc next 10 dc, dc2tog. 12 sts

Rounds 66–67: Dc around. 12 sts Complete stuffing.

Fasten off, leaving a long tail.

Muzzle

Round 1: Using C and MC, work 5 dc. 5 sts

Round 2: 2dc into each st. 10 sts

Round 3: (2dc in next dc, dc in next dc) rep around. 15 sts

Round 4: (2dc in next dc, dc in next 2 dc) rep around. 20 sts

Rounds 5–9: Dc around. 20 sts

Break yarn, leaving a long tail.

Round	Stitches	Yarn
1	MC 5	C
2	10 (inc 5)	C
3	15 (inc 5)	C
4	20 (inc 5)	C
5–9	20	C

Head

Round 1: Using A and MC, work 5 dc. 5 sts

Round 2: 2dc into each st. 10 sts

Round 3: (2dc in next dc, dc in next dc) rep around. 15 sts

Round 4: (2dc in next dc, dc in next 2 dc) rep around. 20 sts

Round 5: (2dc in next dc, dc in next 3 dc) rep around. 25 sts

Round 6: (2dc in next dc, dc in next 4 dc) rep around. 30 sts

Rounds 7–12: Dc around. 30 sts

Round 13: (dc in next 4 dc, dc2tog) rep around. 25 sts

Round 14: (dc in next 3 dc, dc2tog) rep around. 20 sts

Break yarn, leaving a long tail.

Round	Stitches	Yarn
1	MC 5	A
2	10 (inc 5)	A
3	15 (inc 5)	A
4	20 (inc 5)	A
5	25 (inc 5)	A
6	30 (inc 5)	A
7–12	30	A
13	25 (dec 5)	A
14	20 (dec 5)	A

Main fin

Round 1: Using C, work 7ch, turn.

Rounds 2–9: Dc around.

Fold in half and join together thus: (5ch, dc into next set of sts); rep to form a series of loops along edge.

Small fin (make 4)

Round 1: Using C and MC, work 3 dc. 3 sts

Round 2: 2dc into each st. 6 sts

Round 3: (2dc in next dc, dc in next dc) rep around. 9 sts

Round 4: (dc in next dc, dc2tog) rep around. 6 sts

Break yarn, leaving a long tail.

Medium fin (make 2)

Round 1: Using C and MC, work 4 dc. 4 sts

Round 2: 2dc into each dc. 8 sts

Round 3: (2dc in next dc, dc in next dc) rep around. 12 sts

Round 4: (dc in next dc, dc2tog) rep around. 8 sts

Break yarn, leaving a long tail.

Making up

Embroider mouth. Stuff muzzle and partly attach to head. Attach eyes and stuff head. Finish sewing on muzzle. Sew head to body. Sew main fin to middle of body and medium fins to either side. Attach small fins to head and tail. Curl tail slightly and sew to form shape.

Cuddly sheep are always a firm favourite with children, and this little fellow is no exception. He's the perfect bedtime companion to help with counting sheep.

Simon Sheep

Materials

Sirdar Snuggly Snowflake DK 100% polyester (85m per 25g)

2 x 25g balls white (A)

Debbie Bliss Cashmerino Aran 55% merino wool 33% microfibre 12% cashmere (90m per 50g)

25g black (B)

4mm and 4.5mm crochet hooks

Polyester stuffing

Embroidery thread

Toy eyes

Special techniques

Magic circle (MC)

Double crochet (dc)

Increasing

Decreasing

Size

6in (15cm) from nose to tail

Head

Round 1: Using 4mm hook, B and MC, work 6 dc. 6 sts

Round 2: 2dc into each st. 12 sts

Round 3: (2dc in next dc, dc in next dc) rep around. 18 sts

Round 4: (2dc in next dc, dc in next 2 dc) rep around. 24 sts

Round 5: (2dc in next dc, dc in next 3 dc) rep around. 30 sts

Rounds 6–11: Dc around. 30 sts

Round 12: (dc in next 3 dc, dc2tog) rep around. 24 sts

Round 13: (dc in next 2 dc, dc2tog) rep around. 18 sts

Stuff head.

Round 14: (dc in next dc, dc2tog) rep around. 12 sts

Round 15: (dc2tog) rep around. 6 sts

Work 2 sts into 1 until hole closes.

Fasten off.

Round	Stitches	Yarn
1	MC 6	B
2	12 (inc 6)	B
3	18 (inc 6)	B
4	24 (inc 6)	B
5	30 (inc 6)	B
6–11	30	B
12	24 (dec 6)	B
13	18 (dec 6)	B
	Stuff	
14	12 (dec 6)	B
15	6 (dec 6)	B

Body

Round 1: Using 4.5mm hook, two strands of A and MC, work 5 dc. 5 sts

Round 2: 2dc into each st. 10 sts

Round 3: (2dc in next dc, dc in next dc) rep around. 15 sts

Round 4: (2dc in next dc, dc in next 2 dc) rep around. 20 sts

Round 5: (2dc in next dc, dc in next 3 dc) rep around. 25 sts

Round 6: Dc around. 25 sts

Round 7: (2dc in next dc, dc in next 4 dc) rep around. 30 sts

Rounds 8–14: Dc around. 30 sts

Round 15: (dc in next 4 dc, dc2tog) rep around. 25 sts

Round 16: Dc around (25 sts)

Round 17: (dc in next 3 dc, dc2tog) rep around. 20 sts

Round 18: (dc in next 2 dc, dc2tog) rep around. 15 sts

Stuff body.

Round 19: (dc in next dc, dc2tog) rep around. 10 sts

Round 20: (dc2tog) rep around. 5 sts

Work 2 sts into 1 until hole closes.

Round	Stitches	Yarn
1	MC 5	A
2	10 (inc 5)	A
3	15 (inc 5)	A
4	20 (inc 5)	A
5	25 (inc 5)	A
6	25	A
7	30 (inc 5)	A
8–14	30	A
15	25 (dec 5)	A
16	25	A
17	20 (dec 5)	A
18	15 (dec 5)	A
	Stuff body	
19	10 (dec 5)	A
20	5 (dec 5)	A

Legs (make 4)

Round 1: Using 4mm hook and B, work 5 dc. 5 sts

Round 2: 2dc into each st. 10 sts

Rounds 3–5: Dc around. 10 sts

Change to A.

Rounds 6–9: Using two strands of A, dc around. 10 sts

Break yarn, leaving a long tail.

Stuff.

Round	Stitches	Yarn
1	MC 5	B
2	10 (inc 5)	B
3–5	10	B
6–9	10	A

Tail

Round 1: Using 4.5mm hook, two strands of A and MC, work 4 dc. 4 sts

Round 2: 2dc into each st. 8 sts

Rounds 3–5: Dc around. 8 sts
Break yarn, leaving a long tail.
Stuff.

Round	Stitches	Yarn
1	MC 4	A
2	8 (inc 4)	A
3–5	8	A

Head top piece

Round 1: Using 4.5mm hook, two strands of A and MC, work 6 dc. 6 sts

Round 2: 2dc into each st. 12 sts

Round 3: (2dc in next dc, dc in next dc) rep around. 18 sts

Round 4: (2dc in next dc, dc in next 2 dc) rep around. 24 sts

Round 5: (2dc in next dc, dc in next 3 dc) rep around. 30 sts
Fasten off.

Round	Stitches	Yarn
1	MC 6	A
2	12 (inc 6)	A
3	18 (inc 6)	A
4	24 (inc 6)	A
5	30 (inc 6)	A

Ears (make 2)

Round 1: Using 4mm hook, B and MC, work 4 dc. 4 sts

Round 2: 2dc into each st. 8 sts

Round 3: (2dc in next dc, dc in next dc) rep around. 12 sts

Round 4: Dc around. 12 sts

Round 5: (dc in next 2 dc, dc2tog) rep around. 8 sts

Rounds 6–7: Dc around. 8 sts
Fasten off, leaving a long tail.

Round	Stitches	Yarn
1	MC 4	B
2	8 (inc 4)	B
3	12 (inc 4)	B
4	12	B
5	8 (dec 4)	B
6–7	8	B

Making up

Sew head top piece to main head piece, easing to fit, and attach ears to head. Attach eyes and embroider mouth. Sew head to body. Attach tail.

A cuddly crocheted creation!

Techniques

How to make your lovely Amigurumi

What is Amigurumi?

Amigurumi is the art of knitting or crocheting small stuffed animals or anthropomorphic creatures. The word derives from the Japanese words *ami*, meaning crocheted or knitted, and *nuigurumi*, meaning stuffed doll.

Amigurumi creatures are made from yarn that is worked with a smaller size of hook than is usual for the weight of yarn. This produces a closely-woven fabric without any gaps through which stuffing might escape. Amigurumi are usually worked in sections and joined, though some designs may have a head and torso but no limbs, and be worked in one piece.

The simplest Amigurumi designs are worked in spirals, but unlike traditional Western crochet, which is usually made in joined rounds, the various parts are made individually, then stuffed and sewn together. A typical Amigurumi toy will consist of an over-sized round head, a cylindrical body, arms and legs, plus ears and tail if appropriate. The body is usually stuffed with fibre stuffing, while limbs and other extremities are sometimes stuffed with plastic pellets to give them a lifelike weight. Safety eyes may be used, or the features may simply be embroidered on the toy. Felt is often used to create the ears, face, or nose, and it may also be used to make cute embellishments.

Welcome to the world of Amigurumi!

Crochet

Crocheting is a method of creating fancy lacy patterns using yarn and a single hook. Little is known of its history, and the earliest known examples date only from the 18th century, when it first became popular in Europe. It may have evolved from traditional craft practices in Arabia, South America or China.

Originally we were knitters, and taught ourselves how to crochet from a book. We now agree that crocheting is far easier than knitting; it is simply pulling yarn through a loop. Another appealing factor is the speed of crochet, and it is convenient when travelling: no need to worry about needles poking from your bag at rush hour, or dropped stitches!

The fabric produced by crochet is different from knitted fabric. Knitting produces regular stitches and a fabric that is usually quite stretchy. Crochet, however, produces stitches that are more compact, so the resulting fabric is denser and less stretchy. The qualities of crochet fabric mean that it is perfect for making Amigurumi.

Crochet hooks

Traditional crochet hooks range from a bent needle in a cork handle to expensively-crafted silver, brass, steel, ivory and bone hooks. Modern hooks are usually made from aluminium, plastic or steel, but are also available in wood and bamboo.

For Amigurumi, we recommend aluminium or steel hooks. We often work with pieces that require tight, dense stitches and find metal hooks easier to use as they slip more easily between the stitches. We can also pull on them as much as we like without worrying that they will snap! The obvious disadvantage of metal hooks is that they are cold to the touch and can be very slippery, so choose what you feel comfortable with. For projects that require larger hooks or very thick yarn, it may be worth experimenting with wooden hooks as they are not as slippery as metal hooks and are available in beautiful designs.

Hooks are sized according to thickness, and the size is identified in millimetres or by a letter (US). In this book, we use hooks between 2.5mm and 5mm, but any size can be used, depending on the thickness of the yarn. Remember that the smaller the hook, the tighter and denser the stitches. Tight, dense stitches are what you want to achieve, though not so tight that they are impossible to work! As a rough guide, hooks sized from 3–3.5mm are suitable for most cashmere-mix or acrylic Aran yarn.

Just to make things a little more interesting, there are US and UK abbreviations for crochet. This book uses the UK name double crochet (dc) rather than the UK single crochet (sc).

Choosing yarn

There are three main choices when considering yarn for Amigurumi projects: colour, weight and yarn type. Beside these important choices, we also look at the practical care of your precious creations.

With children in mind, we have tried to make everything washable and easy to care for, leaving you more time to create more projects. We mainly used Aran-weight yarn in various blends including cashmere and merino wool, acrylic or cotton. These yarns are durable and give a solid finish, which helps the finished toy to hold its shape. These yarn types are twisted, so the strands are less likely to unravel, and they are also easier to work when you are using a small hook.

Colour

There are two main approaches to selecting the right colour yarn for your project: by using contrasting colours, or by using complementary colours. Contrasting colours typically work well for 'bold' projects with large pieces to make up and contrast. Complementary colours and softer shades such as pastels work well for more 'delicate' projects and smaller pieces. There are no rights or wrongs, so mix and match as you like to make your work unique.

Colourfastness

It is a good idea to choose a yarn that is colourfast, especially if the finished item is intended for a child. Modern yarn is colourfast, but yarn produced by traditional dyeing methods may not be.

For projects made in multiple shades it is particularly important to test for colourfastness, to ensure that a dark colour will not run into a pale colour. To test, simply wet a piece of the yarn, wrap tightly round a piece of white paper towel and allow to dry. Unwind the yarn, and if the towel has changed colour the yarn is not colourfast and may need to be dry cleaned.

Yarn structure

Yarns are made up of thin strands of spun fibre, twisted together to make up the required thickness. The twist is another important consideration: with some yarns the twist quickly unravels if you make a few mistakes and need to undo and rework. Choose a yarn with a firm twist that is less likely to unravel during the process.

Yarn weight

Yarns are generally classified into different types (see chart). We have mainly used yarns in light and medium weights (DK and Aran) for our projects.

Yarn weight	Yarn type
lace	2-ply
super fine	3-ply *(US fingering)*
fine	4-ply *(US sport); sock; baby, quickerknit; lightweight DK*
light	DK *(US light worsted)*
medium	Aran *(US fisherman/worsted); Afghan*
heavy	Chunky *(US bulky)*
very heavy	Super chunky *(US extra-bulky)*

Yarn type

The range of available yarns has grown with new technology, which has allowed different fibres to be spun and twisted into yarn. Different fibres have varying properties, so the various yarns will be suitable for different types of projects.

Wool

This warm, breathable natural fibre is very popular. Most wool yarn comes from the fleeces of sheep but is also produced from the wool of some breeds of goat, llama, camel and rabbit. It is very easy to work and its elasticity is useful if your tension is uneven.

Cotton

This plant fibre is available in varying grades of softness. Cotton is very kind to the skin and is suitable for people with skin allergies. It takes dye well, and produces beautiful strong colours. It also washes well.

Silk

This yarn is produced from the cocoons of various kinds of silk moth. Collecting and spinning the silk fibres is a time-consuming job, hence the high cost of silk yarn. Silk-mix yarns may be a cost-effective alternative.

Mixed fibres

Many different textures and weights of yarn are available in a wide range of fibres that are mixed for their different qualities and properties.

Environmentally friendly

Natural fibre yarns including soya and bamboo are increasingly popular.

Novelty

These yarns are usually spun from man-made fibres, and are often made up of several plies or strands of yarn that are twisted together.

Materials

Apart from yarn and hooks, the craft of Amigurumi requires relatively few materials. Each project will be an individual creation, and the personalisation will come in your finishing touches. Our designs should be regarded as a springboard for your own ideas; with this in mind, these are some of the additional materials you may need.

Stuffing

We used Minicraft Supersoft Toy Stuffing, which conforms to BS1425, BN5852 and EN71 standards and is safe for children. It is washable, can be used in all types of toy making, and is readily available in good craft stores as well as online.

Tapestry needle

These have rounded tips, and will be used to stitch or join the different parts of your Amigurumi. As an alternative to using embellishments, your finished toy may also be embroidered.

Felt

Felt may be used to make eyes and other embellishments for Amigurumi. The advantage of felt is that it is available in a wide assortment of colours, so it is ideal for making your project individual. The disadvantage is that felt may run; if in doubt, check for colour-fastness or use another material. If you want to make a toy that is easily laundered, substitute scraps of any washable fabric as a child-friendly alternative to felt.

Eyes

Many different types of toy eyes are available, including safety eyes that are secured on the inside of the toy using washers, sewn-on eyes and eyes that may be attached using adhesive. Most of the projects in this book use safety eyes, or have eyes embroidered using embroidery thread, because these are the most child-friendly options.

Embroidery thread

You will need an assortment of different-coloured threads to add detail to your work. Amigurumi may be personalised by embroidering features and patterns, and as your confidence increases you will really be able to discover your creative side.

Crochet techniques

Chain stitch

1 With the hook in the right hand and the yarn resting over the middle finger of the left hand, pull the yarn taut. Take the hook under, then over yarn.

2 Pull the hook and yarn through the loop, holding the slip knot steady. Repeat action to form an even chain.

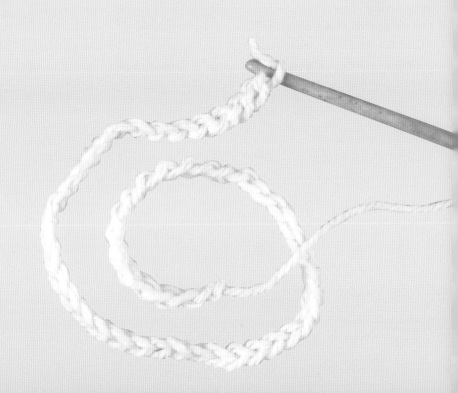

Double crochet

1 Place the hook into a stitch. Wrap the yarn round the hook and draw it back through the stitch towards you; there should now be two loops on the hook.

2 Wrap the yarn round the hook again, then draw it through both loops so there is one loop left on the hook. Repeat across the row.

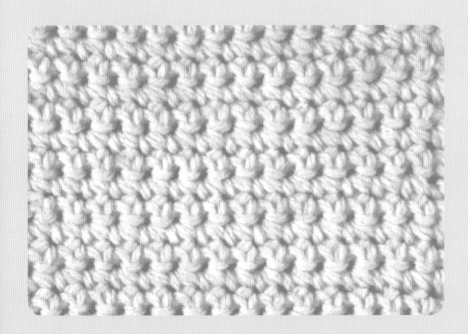

Magic circle technique

Many crochet patterns begin by working a chain of stitches and linking them in a ring with a slip stitch. This may leave an unsightly hole, depending on how many chain stitches you begin with. For small, neat work like Amigurumi, this is not ideal as it may spoil the look of the finished toy.

A better method is to begin by using the magic circle technique, in which stitches are worked over a loop of yarn. The loop is then pulled taut and fastened off, leaving no hole. The step-by-step photographs below will help you to work your first magic circle.

Making the loop

1 Wrap the yarn around your fingers to form a ring.

2 Insert the hook and pick up a loop of yarn.

3 Take yarn over hook and pull though to form a loop.

Working into the ring

4 Insert the hook into the ring…

5 …wrap yarn round hook…

6 … and pull through ring so there are 2 loops on the hook.

7 Wrap yarn round hook again wand pull through both loops…

8 … to complete the first dc.

9 Continue in dc round the ring.

Joining the ring

10 Insert hook into the first stitch.

11 Wrap yarn round hook.

12 Pull through the stitch and the loop already on the hook.

13 Now pull the hanging tail...

14 ... to close the ring.

 **15** Continue in dc…

16a … pulling yarn through stitches of previous row…

16b … and wrapping yarn round hook as before …

16c … to increase size of ring.

Changing colours

To ensure a good finish for your creations, it is important to practise changing colours neatly and efficiently.

Begin dc in the normal way by inserting the hook into the stitch, wrapping the yarn round and pulling through.

1 Now wrap the second colour round the hook…

2 … and pull through both loops of the first colour. Tie yarn ends to prevent them escaping as you work.

3 Using the second colour of yarn, dc into next stitch.

4 Repeat step 3.

5 The completed colour change.

Increasing and decreasing

Decreasing

1 Insert hook into stitch, wrap yarn round and pull through.

2 Insert hook into next stitch, wrap yarn, and pull through.

3 The hook should contain 3 loops.

4 Complete the decrease by wrapping yarn around hook and pulling through all 3 loops…

5 … to complete the decrease, also known as 2 sts into 1.

Increasing

Work 2 dc into the same stitch.

Amigurumi spirals

Some amigurumi patterns give the instructions in the form of diagrams showing the spirals to be worked. We think it is easier to work from simple row-by-row charts, so you know exactly where you are at any time, and how many stitches on each row.

It is easy to count the number of rows that you have worked on any piece of amigurumi: just count the ridges produced by the rows of double crochet stitches. To determine where a row begins or ends, start with the end of yarn left when making the initial magic circle and count vertically. If you

are worried about this, you can use a contrast thread or stitch markers to delineate the beginning of the rows.

The illustrations that follow show how the instructions for Zelda Zebra's muzzle and body can be rendered as spiral diagrams.

Muzzle spiral

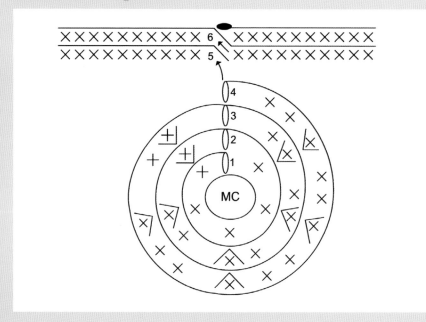

Body spiral

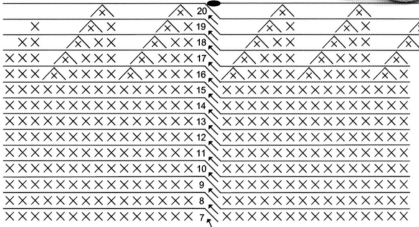

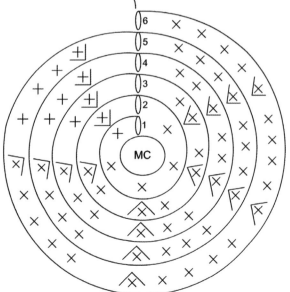

Sewing up

This is an important stage, as you do not want all your hard work to be ruined by a toy that falls apart. Most of the stuffing and sewing up necessary for your Amigurumi will be done as you go along, so there will be no need for major assembly at the end.

Sewing up is usually done using the yarn ends left when the initial magic circle is made. Using a darning needle, take small, neat stitches and try to make them show as little as possible. Fasten off yarn ends securely by taking several stitches through your work.

1 Stuff the neck of the toy firmly, then attach it using small, neat stitches all round.

2 Take care to maintain the circular shape of the top of the limbs when sewing on.

Blanket stitch

Work from left to right. The twisted edge should lie on the outer edge of the fabric to form a raised line. Bring needle up at point **A**, down at **B** and up at **C** with thread looped under the needle. Pull through. Take care to tighten the stitches equally. Repeat to the right. Fasten the last loop by taking a small stitch along the lower line.

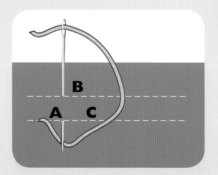

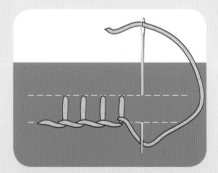

Conversions

Crochet chart symbols

The symbols shown are those traditionally used in instructions for working Amigurumi.

Symbol	UK term	US term	Japanese
✕	dc (double crochet)	sc (single crochet)	こま編み
⋎	2dc inc	2-sc inc *(2-single crochet increase)*	増目（こま編 み2目編み入れ）
⋏	2 sts into 1	2-sc dec *(2-single crochet cluster/decrease)*	減目（こま編 み2目1度）

UK/US yarn weights

UK	US
2–ply	Lace
3–ply	Fingering
4–ply	Sport
Double knitting	Light worsted
Aran	Fisherman/worsted
Chunky	Bulky
Super chunky	Extra bulky

Hook conversions

UK	Metric	US
14	2mm	B/1
13	2.25mm	–
12	2.5mm	C/2
11	3mm	–
10	3.25mm	D/3
9	3.5mm	E/4
8	4mm	G/6
7	4.5mm	–
6	5mm	H/8
5	5.5mm	I/9
4	6mm	J/10

Note: check tension and use a larger/smaller hook if necessary

Abbreviations

approx	approximately	**dec**	decrease	**patt**	pattern
alt	alternate	**foll**	following	**rem**	remaining
beg	beginning	**g**	gramme(s)	**rep**	repeat
C	contrast (colour)	**in(s)**	inch(es)	**RS**	right side of work
ch	chain	**inc**	increase	**sl st**	slip stitch
cm(s)	centimetre (s)	**m**	metre	**st(s)**	stitches
cont	continue	**M**	main (colour)	**tog**	together
Dc	double crochet	**MC**	magic circle technique	**WS**	wrong side of work
Dc2tog	double crochet 2 sts together to decrease	**mm**	millimetre	**yds**	yards

Index

The art of Amigurumi

THIS BOOK IS THE RESULT OF A HOBBY shared by best friends, Lan-Anh and Josephine. Lan-Anh first discovered Amigurumi as a fun pastime and a way of making gifts for friends, including Josephine's toddler son Lewis.

When Lan-Anh gave Josephine a cute dog she had made, she wanted to make some Amigurumi of her own. As a beginner in crochet she was worried about her chances of success, but it was such fun and so easy that in just two weeks she had learned the basic techniques and was soon making some amazing creatures.

If you struggle to complete your knitted projects – does a sweater without arms sound familiar? – Amigurumi is for you. It can be extremely addictive, and you are so eager to see the result of your efforts that the toys are completed very quickly.

Amigurumi became yet another thing the friends had in common, and they often stayed up until the small hours making toys and planning the next project. Friends and family were so impressed by the results that they could not wait to see the next creation. It was soon clear that Amigurumi was not just for children.

If you love making things but have little time, Amigurumi could be the answer. It is not only easily manageable but very portable: Lan-Anh may make an ear on the train, and legs on the bus! A visit to Japan provided lots of ideas and inspiration for new designs and projects, and the idea for this book was born.

Lan-Anh

Josephine and Lewis

155

To place an order, or to request a catalogue, contact:

GMC Publications Ltd

Castle Place, 166 High Street, Lewes, East Sussex, BN7 1XU

United Kingdom

Tel: + 44 (0) 1273 488005

Website: www.gmcbooks.com

Orders by credit card are accepted